Billy Sunday
Baseball Preacher

Billy Sunday
Baseball Preacher

by
Fern Neal Stocker

MOODY PRESS

CHICAGO

© 1985 by
THE MOODY BIBLE INSTITUTE
OF CHICAGO

Library of Congress Cataloging in Publication Data

Stocker, Fern Neal, 1917-
    Billy Sunday, baseball preacher.

    Summary: Recounts the story of a professional baseball
player who dedicated his life to spreading the gospel,
with emphasis on his childhood in Iowa in the 1870s.
    1. Sunday, Billy, 1862-1935—Juvenile literature.
2. Evangelists—United States—Biography—Juvenile
literature.   3. Baseball players—United States—
Biography—Juvenile literature.   [1. Sunday, Billy,
1862-1935.   2. Evangelists.   3. Baseball players]
I. Title.
BV3785.S8S76   1985   269'.2'0924 [B] [92]   84-25488
ISBN 0-8024-0442-1 (pbk.)

1 2 3 4 5 6 7 Printing/LC/Year 88 87 86 85

Printed in the United States of America

*To the wonderful children attending
the Curtis Baptist School in
Augusta, Georgia*

Contents

1

Cobs and Chips

"**M**a, I want to go swimming!" said Willie one hot June day in 1873. "Can't you hear the big boys yelling over at Squaw Creek? Please, Ma, please!"

"No, Willie, you can't swim, and it's baking day. You must bring in cobs and chips," replied Mother. "Besides, you know how your Grandfather Corley feels about those indecent swimming suits the boys wear nowadays. Why, they go up past their knees and have no arms at all. You boys will never have suits like that. One thing, we haven't money for store-bought clothes; and another, I could never face your grandfather! You just hustle about and bring in the cobs and chips. That will keep you busy all morning!"

Willie knew it was no use arguing with his mother. She always did what Grandfather Corley said. He guessed it was because Squire Corley helped out in the place of his father, who had died

9

in the war. Willie wished he had known his father, but all he had were two old, faded pictures.

Since he couldn't argue, Willie went out to the barn. The corn cobs were easy to get, because they were saved at "corn husking" time. There were always piles and piles of cobs. It was amazing all the uses that could be found for them.

He filled the pan half full of corn cobs and then went to the barnyard for the chips. You had to be absolutely sure the cow manure chips were completely dry before picking them up. Using a stick he poked this pile and that pile before picking up any. They really made a hot fire. The only trouble was that it took so many!

Willie's battered dishpan with holes in it was not large enough to hold all the cobs and chips needed for the baking. As Willie brought in the first panful he noticed the woodbox was empty. Edward, his older brother, was supposed to keep it full, but as usual Edward could not be found.

When he returned to the yard, he said to his dog, "Watch, if I could fill the woodbox without Mother noticing, I could twenty-three skiddoo like Edward, and Mother would have enough fuel for the baking too." He knew the woodbox was for wood, not for cobs and chips, but what matter? Everyone said Willie's legs flew like greased lightning, and that helped. When he noticed Mother looking around, he brought in another pan of cobs and chips, which she used. He took the pan again, and this time he finished filling the woodbox. Then he brought another panful to set beside the stove.

Since he knew that would be enough, he ducked out of the kitchen, down the path to Squire Corley's Squaw Creek. He always ran over the squire's property as if it were his own. He knew the squire loved him in spite of his stern words. But he hoped the squire would not attend the swimming party today.

What a sight it was to see the boys splashing and swimming! It was true, some had on those indecent bathing suits, but many of them had taken them off and were swimming in the buff. He decided if he did that his mother would never know he had been swimming, since his clothes would be dry. He did not see one boy's father sleeping under a bush nearby or he may have been more careful.

Willie knew he did not know how to swim, and he had been told repeatedly that Squaw Creek had "drop-offs" in it—places where the shallow water suddenly was six, eight, or even ten feet deep. He had heard stories of drownings, but who could think of that on a beautiful sunny day in June?

In Willie jumped. What fun to be laughing, splashing, and kicking water at the big boys. He picked up shells on the sand bar. He noticed many of the older boys were careful to stay close to the bank, too. They must not know how to swim either, he decided.

Yes, just as he thought—Edward was there, not caring that his woodbox was full of cobs and chips instead of wood. He yelled at Willie.

"Willie, you shouldn't be here! You know you're too young."

"I'm old enough, smarty! Plenty old enough to learn to sw—" He never finished the sentence. Down he went into a drop-off.

Willie had always heard that you went down three times into the deep water before you drowned. With a mouthful of water Willie kicked and splashed, trying to help himself. He managed to come to the surface, frantically trying to call out "Help!" but he never could get out the word before he went down again. All the boys began screaming and pointing. The father napping under the bush suddenly woke up. He looked where the boys were pointing and saw Willie come up for the third time. Willie gasped, sputtered, screamed, and then sank to the bottom. He asked forgiveness for disobeying his mother by coming swimming. When the man's arms reached him he was completely unconscious.

What a time the boys had with Willie. The father held him by the feet to let the water drain out of his mouth. They laid him on his back and worked his arms up and down to start him breathing again. They started to carry him home when he came to himself and said, "I want to go to Mamma. Oh, I'm so sick to my stomach! E-yah-ah!" And up came a lot of water.

As he was being carried down the path with

the sober-faced boys trailing behind, he heard his mother calling, "Willie! Willie!" At that the boys in the buff suddenly turned and ran, leaving the others to carry Willie into the shack and put him to bed.

After covering him with kisses and hugs, his mother also covered his chest with a plaster. She kept saying, "It's a miracle, God saved you! God saved you for a reason. God wants you to do something for Him! Oh, Willie, be thankful! Never refuse to do anything God asks of you. He saved you for something—find out what it is and do it, my boy! Do it!"

Then she sang as Willie dozed, "Where He leads me I will follow, where He leads me I will follow. I'll go with Him, with Him all the way."

"Ma," said Willie, "I prayed when I was drowning, I really did."

"Yes, Willie," replied his mother. "Nothing improves the prayer life like trouble. Now before you go to sleep say your prayers, dear."

So Willie repeated the prayer he had said every night as long as he could remember.

> "Jesus, bless this little lamb,
> Weak and sinful though I am.
> Lead me, guide me, day by day;
> Never let me from Thee stray."

After he had asked God's blessing on everyone he silently thanked God for saving his life. "There must be something You want me to do with it," he said sleepily. "I wonder what it is."

2

School Days

"**W**hy do you start school late every year?" demanded Egbert as Edward and Willie reported three weeks late the fall of 1873.

"Because we have to get the shocking and thrashing done first, that's why," responded Willie.

"Our hired man always does that kind of work on our farm," boasted Egbert.

"Well, we don't need no hired man on our place," retorted Willie. "Edward and I each do a man's work in the fields. This is the second year I've been holding a man's place. Grandfather says that's real good for a ten-year-old."

"It's child labor, my dad says—"

"Oh, mind your own beeswax," retorted Willie, walking into the schoolhouse.

Miss Miller smiled at the boys.

"Come on in, boys. I'm glad you came before time to take up classes because I want to give you your books and get you started," she said.

"Tell me about what you have been doing."

"All we've been doing is work," stammered Willie. He wished Edward would answer these questions, but he never did.

"Well, tell me about the work, then. I understand you helped with shocking the grain. How do you do it?" urged Miss Miller.

It occurred to Willie that maybe Miss Miller, who knew everything else, didn't know about shocking. Imagine, a teacher, too!

"Every morning I get the team ready," he explained. "Then Grandfather drives the binder through the fields and cuts the grain. Edward comes next and ties the grain into armbundles with twine. He's good at tying knots, you can bet. Then I come behind him and stack three bundles on end into shocks so the rain runs off and the wheat doesn't get wet. When it's all shocked we bring in the wagon and use a pitchfork to load it to take to the grinding mill. That's all we did, Miss Miller."

"My! That must have been hard work. Didn't you get tired?"

"Sure we did, but Grandfather said you weren't supposed to get tired until you were finished. We were all ready to drop dead when the day was over. Ma don't think Grandfather can do it another year."

By that time Miss Miller had two stacks of books placed on a double desk for the boys.

Willie eyed his fourth *McGuffey's Eclectic Reader*. It was blue and mustard color. He gave it a flip and noticed the first pages—every kind of vocals, subvocals, and aspirates. He groaned within himself. He remembered Egbert's being praised for reciting all those sounds last year. There was no way out. Miss Miller never let you go on to page 2 until you recited page 1 perfectly—not if it took forever.

He noticed a thirteen-verse poem called "Strawberries," and his heart sank. *What could anyone say about strawberries that would take thirteen verses?* he wondered. But he knew he'd never get to read page 74 until hs finished reciting "Strawberries" on page 73. Miss Miller meant for you to learn it perfectly. No wonder that Wilbur, at fourteen, was still in the fourth reader. Willie thought, *I don't want to be like that.*

Miss Miller took the school bell from her desk, stood at the door, and rang it.

Willie and Edward went back outside so they could march in. They knew their places from last year. The first grade—there were only two pupils—went first, then each grade in turn so they looked like twenty-six stairsteps marching in. All eight grades were present. The other two fourth-graders were already three weeks ahead of Willie. He knew he would have to work hard to catch up.

When Willie had been in the field shocking, he had dreamed of sitting quietly in school at his desk with nothing to do but study. It had seemed heavenly then, but now he wondered if shocking was not easier after all.

17

Miss Miller began the day by reading *Jack Ward* to the pupils. It had just been published that summer, and Miss Miller was happy to have a new story by Horatio Alger, the children's favorite author.

After the story, lessons began. First the little first-graders were called up. They took their slates and showed Miss Miller their letters. She had marked them in chalk, and the children had laid corn kernels over the chalk marks. They said, "C says *Ca*," and drew a C in the air. As Willie listened he decided he had better learn his punctuation marks or he wouldn't have anything to recite when the fourth grade was called upon to go up.

"The hyphen is used in the dictionary between syllables and between the parts of a compound word: no-ble, col-o-ny; and text-books or easy-chair." Willie repeated the words over and over, pounding his head when he forgot a word. He wondered how long it would be until recess. Recess was his favorite time.

When Miss Miller said "Turn," they all put their legs in the aisle; "Stand," everyone stood; "Pass," and they all marched by rows out the door. The order was very good, for they knew if it were not Miss Miller would make them repeat it all recess.

"Let's play Pom Pom Pullaway," Egbert yelled.

"Or Red Rover, or Fox and Hound," someone else added.

18

"No, not that!" several clamored.

The girls decided to jump rope.

"Lady, lady, turn around,
Lady, Lady, touch the ground,
Lady, Lady touch your shoe
Lady, Lady, twenty-three skiddoo."

Other girls were chanting: "Salt! Pepper! Vinegar! Mustard! Hot!" They turned the rope faster and faster.

The boys looked at each other. Then Timmy called out, "Let's play Duck on a Rock." They all ran to a post that was sometimes used to hitch horses. One of them put a large rock on top of the post. The rest of the boys scurried about, yelling and searching for rocks for the game. They lined up to take turns throwing rocks at the "duck." One rock moved the duck a bit, another shook it almost off the post. Finally Edward knocked it off and became the winner. Before the recess was over there were six winners.

"I'm going to have to practice that game," Willie said to himself. "Those older boys are plenty good."

"Would have been more fun if we'd played Pom Pom Pullaway," mumbled Egbert as they marched back into the classroom.

"Oh, get off your high horse," someone muttered back.

"Quiet there," Miss Miller called out. "You have too much frolic on the brain. Now let's get to work. I mean NOW!" When Miss Miller spoke like that, everyone settled down quickly. They studied so they could recite the next period. She had listened to four grades by lunchtime.

Lunch period went by swiftly. All the children had brought their lunches, most in five-pound lard pails. Sandwiches of thick homemade bread and a jar of milk were the usual fare. They sometimes also had apples. Lunch time was "their" time. In fact, they liked to think this was their time to talk without the teacher listening.

Miss Miller didn't mind. She usually did her janitor work at noon. She swept the floor and in the winter tended the fire. She always welcomed help with cleaning the blackboard or erasers.

But all too soon it was time to get back to work. If Miss Miller listened to three grades before afternoon recess, Willie knew she was planning something special for the last hour.

Sometimes she let them draw with charcoal on big sheets of paper; sometimes they did drills with Indian clubs or wands; sometimes they would take pen and ink and practice ovals and push and pulls in their copybooks. These exercises were supposed to make their hands loose when they wrote their letters.

Once in a while they had "spelldowns" or "figure downs." Willie could do very well in the spelling bees, but he had a hard time when it came to figuring arithmetic in his head.

Most fun of all were the rare days they ran races. Miss Miller kept track of their times with her big watch. "Willie runs faster than greased lightning," she always said. Of course, Willie liked race days best. It was the one time he was always a winner.

All week the youngsters worked to get every lesson learned by Friday noon, because Friday afternoons were reserved for recitations. Each one had to do something or recite something.

One Friday Timmy Brown created a riot by reciting, "Lincoln was a great man; Washington also was a great man; but here, my friends, is a greater." He then held up a cheese grater. His friends thought they could never stop laughing.

Willie became famous one Friday by reciting a poem his Grandmother found for him.

Ain't I Glad I Ain't a Girl

Ain't I glad I ain't a girl,
Hands to wash and hair to curl,
Skirts a-flappin 'round my knees,
Ain't I glad that that ain't me?

Grandpa says it's just a chance
That I got to wearing pants,
Says that when a kid is small
They put dresses on 'em all.

They that kicks and makes a noise
Gets promoted into boys.
Them that sits and twists their curls,
They just leaves them, calls them "girls."

Parents, grandparents, aunts, uncles, and friends all hunted for "pieces" the children could learn for Friday afternoons. Everyone in the school had to recite. It was to help them speak properly and not be shy in front of people. At first Willie hated it, but as the years went by he loved holding the attention of the other children. He always tried to find something funny or with a meaning. One he especially liked was:

> Voyagers upon Life's Sea;
>   to yourself be true,
> And whatever your lot may be,
>   Paddle your own canoe.

3

Mother's Surprise

"Co, boss, co, co." Willie directed the cows out of the lane and into the pasture. After putting up the bars at the gate he turned back down the lane toward the farm.

His problem nagged at him. Mother's birthday was tomorrow, and he had no present. Dragging his feet, he looked at the pleasant cornfields, the blue sky, the trees fringing the farm. Nothing helped. As he entered the two-room slatboard shack, Willie confronted his brother, Edward.

"What have you got for Mother's present?" he asked.

"An egg whip. Bought it at the country store," replied Edward. "If you had saved Grandma's Christmas money like I did, you would have a present too."

The fact that Edward was right didn't help. "Oh, so what," Willie answered. "I'm going to make something for Mother. You'll see—she'll like it better than any old egg whip. You'll see!"

"And what are you going to make that's so great?" asked Edward.

Since Willie didn't know, he was slow to answer. But seeing the flour barrel beside the cupboard, he suddenly had an idea. "I'm going to bake bread."

"Bread!—Oh, Willie, how silly can you be? Bread is not easy to make, and you don't know beans about it!"

"Do too," answered Willie. He was tired of his brother, only two years older, saying he didn't know beans about anything. "Mother lets me watch every time she makes it."

"You can't make it puff up and get fluffy like she does," taunted Edward.

"Oh, that's the easiest part," responded Willie. "All you have to do is put in plenty of yeast. I'll put in extra just to be sure."

Edward left the house to Willie, who was so busy he hardly noticed Edward's departure. He also forgot that Mother always made a large fire in the big cookstove before she started making the dough.

Soon Willie's arms and hands were white with flour and lard. He knew everything to put in the mixing bowl, for he had watched his mother a hundred times. True to his word, he put in extra yeast to make sure the bread would rise. Satisfied, he put the dough into the bread pans and set them behind the cold stove. He looked everywhere for a clean white cloth to cover the pans as Mother always did, but couldn't find any.

24

"Doesn't matter anyway," Willie decided.

Then he waited, and waited, wondering if his mother would get back from Squire Corley's before he was ready. He knew he was supposed to say "Grandfather Corley," but since everyone else said "Squire Corley," Willie always thought of him that way.

"This place is a mess." He looked at the blackened chimney glass on the kerosene lantern and decided he could wash it while he was waiting for the dough to rise. Next he saw that the dishes Mother had washed were not put away, so he put them in the dish cupboard near the table. He picked up Mother's book and put it in the dish cabinet, since there was no bookcase. He straightened the straw mats on the table. Mother always set the table and cleaned up just like at Grandma's. Of course, it never looked like Grandma's because their house was so poor and Grandma's was so very grand.

"Why doesn't the dough rise?" Willie looked at it for the hundredth time. "It looks just like it did when I put it in the pan," he said to himself.

Edward came in to get a drink of water. "Oh, Willie!" he moaned. "What did you do to the bread? Why does it look so gray? Didn't you wash your hands before you started kneading it?"

"Oh, sure, find something wrong, would you!" mocked Willie, remembering that he had *not* washed his hands. "Just get out of here! I thought you were going to chop wood!"

"And why is Watch in the house? You know

25

Mother doesn't allow dogs inside."

Willie defended Watch. "He knows he isn't an inside dog. The minute he hears the buggy wheels he will be an outside dog."

"Yeah, yeah," answered Edward, leaving the kitchen.

Willie looked at the bread. He had to admit it had been long enough for it to rise, or at least to get bubbles and puff a little. Doubts began to fill his mind. "Well, I'll wait awhile and see," he told Watch.

He waited and waited—straightening up, watering their one plant, putting clothes away, and making beds, for Willie couldn't be still.

At long last he looked at the dough again. There were four dirty dog prints across the soft surface. "Watch, how could you! Get out of here, you rascal." He threw a shoe at the surprised dog.

Willie looked around. "Well, I've already about cleaned up the place. If I scrubbed the floor, I could say that was Mother's birthday present. But what can I do with the dough so she will never find out?"

"Hateful stuff!" he addressed the soggy, limp, gray dough. "Where can I hide you?"

Looking out the kitchen window, he spied the garden. It didn't take Willie long to dig a very deep hole where some potatoes had been. He did a good job of covering the dough completely. "Now no one will ever know!" he said smugly.

Grinning back at the smooth potato patch, he raced to the kitchen to scrub the floor. Willie was known for being good at scrubbing floors. He took his time. He remembered Squire Corley saying, "People forget how fast you did the job, but they remember how well you did it."

On his knees with a scrub brush, good lye soap, plenty of water in his pail, and a clean rag to wipe up, Willie made the suds fly. It did take a long time, but the floor sparkled. He knew his mother would be pleased. He remembered her saying, "Everything comes to him who waits, if he works while he waits."

"Well, I've been waiting around all morning, but I've been working too, so now I have a present Mother will like." Willie smiled.

However the smile was wiped off Willie's face at the cry, "Earthquake! Earthquake!"

An earthquake—here on the farm in Ames, Iowa. Willie couldn't believe it.

Knocking over his pail of water, Willie tumbled out the door to see what Edward was yelling about.

"I didn't feel anything," Willie was saying as he beheld Edward, frozen stiff, eyes bulging and finger pointing.

The potato patch quivered and shook. Bubbles of white oozed through the black dirt, lifting the clods higher and higher. They rose silently, swelling and cracking the black soil into peculiar shapes and sizes.

Just then Mother drove into the yard with the squire's horse and buggy. Seeing the boys staring, she drove alongside the garden.

"What—what's wrong with the potatoes? Why are they swelling? I never saw potatoes lift the ground and shake! It just can't be. Boys, what is happening?"

Edward was quick to deny knowledge of anything. Mother turned to Willie. "What is it, son? What have you done now?"

Slowly Willie lifted his eyes and the story came out. "I only wanted to surprise you!" he concluded.

Mother looked at the crestfallen boy and back to the dough still bubbling and cracking the dirt. "Oh, you did that, Willie! You will never surprise me more." A slow smile spread over her face as she clasped Willie in her arms.

How could she know this was only the beginning of Willie's surprises?

4

Life with Grandfather

Willie's twelfth year was a time of changes. One day in late summer of 1874, Grandfather Corley called Willie and Edward to a corner of his orchard.

"I want to talk to you boys privately," he said. "I think you should be prepared for what your mother and that Heigler are going to tell you."

Willie picked up his ears. He knew it must be important or his grandfather wouldn't have insisted on this meeting. Few things were that private.

"As you know," began Grandfather, "your mother isn't seeing her other suitor anymore, so they will not be getting married. The worst of it is that she is going to marry Heigler, who isn't— well—anyway, Heigler has suggested that you boys come and live with Grandmother and me." He looked intently at the boys. "Grandmother says, 'It takes both rain and sunshine to make a rainbow,' and she wants you to come and

29

stay with us. It means a sight more work for her. Do you have any questions?"

"Yes, but this might be a dumb question, Grandfather."

"Don't be afraid to ask dumb questions, son. They are easier to handle than dumb mistakes."

"Well, why can't we stay with Mother? Doesn't Mr. Heigler want us?" asked Willie.

"Now, now, I wasn't going to come out and say that, Willie; but if he did want you, I wouldn't hear of it. I've seen how he treats his dog and his horse. You will both be better off with Grandma and me. You will be happy with us. The secret of living is not to do what you like but to like what you have to do. Never forget that, son."

"When will we be moving?" asked Edward. He saw the tears in Willie's eyes and knew Willie couldn't talk anymore.

"Right away," answered Grandfather.

"But it's wrong, it's wrong!" And Willie beat his fists against the tree trunk.

"Willie, it is better to suffer a wrong than to do a wrong. Now you straighten up and don't give your mother trouble when she tells you. That's why I told you before she did. Don't think it is easy for her, either. She loves you both—you know that—but there has to be a man on the farm. I'm just not able to handle two farms and all my work. Anyway, the die is cast, and we will have to live with it."

"But Mother, I'll miss my mother!" cried Willie.

30

"Yes, of course. But mothers are not for leaning on, but for making leaning unnecessary. You are twelve years old now, Willie, and that is old enough to lean on yourself and yourself alone."

"Yes, Grandfather," said Willie. He knew you never argued with Squire Corley, no matter what you thought.

When Mother told the boys, Willie acted like living with Grandfather would be a great life. He only asked one question. "Can Watch go with me?"

His mother said she would not separate him from his beloved dog.

He decided it *was* a good life when Grandfather took him around to all the businesses he operated. The sawmill, where lumber was cut into boards for building, interested Willie. The grain mill, which ground wheat into flour, was fascinating. The sugar mill, turning sugar beets into sugar, caused him to say, "Well, if that don't beat the Dutch!"

Grandfather, how did you ever learn to do so many things?" exclaimed Willie.

"Son, remember I always told you, it is not the man of great natural talent who wins, but he who pushes his talent, however small, to its utmost capacity. Always keep busy. Idle hands are the devil's workshop. That's what I like about you, Willie. You move. You are never still. You'll accomplish much—see if you don't."

Willie was pleased, but he knew he would never match his grandfather's accomplishments.

Grandfather made wagons—the wheels and all parts of them. He could build houses and lay stone walls. He made a turning lathe and made bedposts, water wheels, and even caskets.

Willie also saw his grandfather make horseshoes and wedges with which to split wood in his blacksmith shop. He could dress a millstone to grind corn and wheat. He had even made a loom so Grandmother could weave cloth.

Willie gazed with awe at a letter from President Ulysses S. Grant inviting Squire Corley to spend three weeks in Washington, D.C. "That beats the Dutch!" he exclaimed.

But most of all Willie loved the athletic tricks his grandfather taught him. He showed him how to arm wrestle and win; how to breathe so he could run farther and faster; and how to jump a good distance without wasting energy. He was a better student for the squire than he was at school. Of course, with his grandfather he had to "walk the chalk" for the squire wouldn't stand for any foolishness.

One day Grandfather called Willie to help him. They took a ladder, some beeswax, a big jackknife, a saw, and some cloth into the orchard behind the big house.

Grandfather leaned the ladder against a crabapple tree. He climbed up and sawed off some limbs, split them, and shoved some little pear sprouts as big as his finger into the splits. He tied a string around them after filling the cut with beeswax.

"What are you doing?" inquired Willie.

"I am grafting pear sprouts into the sour crab tree," answered Grandfather.

"Will it grow crab apples or pears now?" asked Willie.

"Pears," said Grandfather thoughtfully. "I don't know if I will ever live to eat the pears, but I know you will."

"I believe we both will, Grandpa," asserted Willie.

Willie was very happy with his grandfather and with Grandmother, too. She would look at him with her clear blue eyes and say, "Happiness comes not from exterior situations but from the peace within you. Joy is never in things—it is within us."

One day Grandma took Willie aside and told him a secret. "I'm telling you, Willie, because I want you to comfort your grandfather. He loves you so much. Willie, I know I will die soon. This weakness has been coming on me for a long, long time. I want you to know I have peace with God, and I'm happy to be going to Him, but I hate leaving your grandfather. I want you to be ready to help him when the time comes."

Willie didn't know what to say or do. He felt strange, and he really didn't believe his grandmother. But when the first of September came, Grandmother died. Willie was stunned. He knew he was supposed to comfort Grandfather, but all he could do was sit near him. He didn't cry or talk. He just sat.

They had a funeral and buried Grandmother in the family graveyard not too far from the house.

The next morning Edward reported that Willie had not slept in their bed. Everyone began searching for him. Finally Grandfather found him lying on Grandmother's grave, sound asleep. Tear stains were on his cheeks. When they woke him he said he felt all right, for while he was there he had remembered all the beautiful things she had told him. He promised himself he would never forget her saying, "Joy is never in things, it is within us."

A few weeks later Mother had a long talk with the boys. "Since Grandmother is gone, there is no one to take care of you, so we are making arrangements to send you to the Soldiers' Orphanage."

Willie was silent.

5

To the Orphanage

Willie and Edward didn't start school when the other children trudged to the classroom that fall. Everyone excused them because of Grandma. But it really wasn't because of Grandma at all. Willie and Edward didn't want anyone to know they were going to the Soldiers' Orphanage.

No new clothes came their way that year. Their old clothes were too small, and the patches Grandmother had put on were worn through. They decided that you must not need clothes at the orphanage. When they looked at Grandfather, he turned his face away. He was so ashamed. They pretended not to see. Men didn't cry, they knew, and especially not Squire Corley.

Mother came and took them down to the hotel where they were to wait for the train to stop. They waited in the lobby. How strange the familiar town looked at midnight with no one moving about. Since Willie had told no one, none of his friends was there to say good-bye.

Edward and Willie slept until about one o'clock in the morning, when someone came for them and said, "Get ready for the train."

Willie looked into his mother's face. Her eyes were red, her hair disheveled. "What's the matter, Mother?" Willie said.

"Oh, son, everything will be all right. I've been praying all the time you were asleep, and I know God will take care of you. 'Out of suffering come the strongest souls. God's wounded often make His best soldiers.' Now you two go to the orphanage, learn all you can, and behave yourselves. Be good, my boys, be good."

When they got to the depot, the train was in. People walked by and didn't say a word. Everyone looked at the crying mother and the wretched boys. No one could think of anything to say. Willie didn't say anything, either. Mother held them and sobbed.

At a sign from the conductor the boys stepped on the stool and hopped up on the step.

"Good-bye, Mother," they called.

After they found a seat the boys looked out the window, and Mother was there, waving and forcing a smile.

"Good-bye, good-bye!" they all cried. The train moved rapidly on its way to Council Bluffs.

Council Bluffs was not their destination. They were to change trains for Glenwood there. But when they arrived in Council Bluffs, they found the train had already left.

"You will have to wait until tomorrow for the next train," they were told.

"Edward, I've just decided something," said Willie.

"It must be bad. You look so sober."

"No, it isn't bad—I've just decided to change my name."

"Ho, ho! The little man doesn't like his name. What better name have you thought up?" Edward laughed.

"I'm going to tell everyone I'm 'Billy.' You know most people named William are called Billy, or even Bill, which would be better."

"But Mother always called you Willie because she called Dad Bill."

"That's true, but now I want to be Bill or at least Billy. It sounds older, and you know I'm going on thirteen now and am no little kid anymore. Please, Edward, you will be the only one at the orphanage that will know the difference. Please, Edward, just say 'Billy.' Please!" pleaded Willie.

"Oh, all right, Billy Boy. Shall I sing, 'Oh, where have you been Billy Boy, Billy Boy? Oh, where have you been, charming Billy?'"

"Cut it out, will you? You know we can't stand and sing on these railroad tracks for a whole day and night. I'm hungry. Come on!"

"Yes, I'm hungry too," said Edward, "but we

don't have any money for food, and you know we can't stay at the hotel. I wish we knew someone in Council Bluffs."

It was cold. The boys turned up the collars on their coats, but they were still shivering. "There's the hotel," Willie said. "Let's walk over there. At least we can get out of the wind. Maybe someone will give us something to eat."

"You mean to beg—to beg!" Edward was astonished.

"No, of course not," replied Willie, "but if someone asks me I'll say, 'Yes, I'm hungry.' I *am*, and you are too."

Willie and Edward pushed their way to the hotel, leaning against the cold wind and holding their faces to the side.

Inside, things were better. They felt propelled toward the dining room. Every smell was just delicious. The bacon frying on the grill sent odors of delight to their souls. The fact that the hotel was old, the stools well worn, the light fixtures dusty was not noticed by the hungry Edward and Willie. They were content to smell and smell.

A very large woman noticed the two boys.

"What's your name?" she asked.

"My name is Billy Sunday, and this is my brother Edward—or Ed, we call him," answered Billy. He had decided to change Edward's name too. Edward was silent.

"Where are you going?" asked the woman.

"Going to the Soldiers' Orphanage at Glenwood," was the reply.

"My husband was a soldier and never came back," choked the woman. "He wouldn't turn you boys away."

She moved to the boys, hugged them both, and invited them into the dining room. She bought their breakfast and invited them back to dinner too.

Feeling better, the boys wandered out into the sunshine. The cold wind had died down. They played around the freight yards, looking at all the trains. Seeing one that looked ready to go their way, they climbed into the caboose.

The conductor came along and asked, "Where is your money?"

"Ain't got any," responded Billy. Edward never said a word.

"Where is your ticket?"

"Ain't got any tickets." Billy shrugged.

"You can't ride without money or tickets. I'll have to put you off the train." The conductor spoke gruffly.

Edward and Billy burst into tears. All their bravery—not crying all the way from Ames to Council Bluffs—all was gone. They both wept.

Edward handed the conductor the letter of introduction he held for the superintendent of the orphan home. The conductor read it and handed it back. With tears in his eyes he said, "Just sit still, boys; it won't cost you a cent to ride on my train."

No one could have been nicer to the boys as they rode along in the caboose. It was only twenty miles from Council Bluffs to Glenwood, and the scenery was beautiful.

As they rounded the last curve going into Glenwood, the conductor said, "There it is on the hill, boys! See your new home! You can easily walk to it from the depot."

The way was short, and although the boys walked as slowly as possible they arrived at the door before they were ready. Billy gritted his teeth and knocked. He remembered Grandfather's saying that you can't do what you like, so you should like what you have to do.

When the door opened Billy said, "My name is Billy Sunday. This is my brother, Ed. He has a letter for the superintendent."

6

Orphanage Life

Living with two hundred boys and girls of all ages was different from living with one brother. At first Edward and Billy just stood around in awe.

They felt awkward because the children were tormenting each other and looking for mischief. They felt awkward because everyone stared at them. Some boys mocked their polite manners and old clothes. But after they got new clothes, they were not noticeable as strangers.

The teachers seemed to be more interested in their behavior than in their learning. It soon became a game. Edward didn't like it, but Billy fit right in. After a few days he was just one of the crowd.

Billy was soon yelling at everyone and running down the halls faster and louder than anyone else. That was how he got into trouble with Mr. F. J. Sessions, superintendent of the orphanage.

Mr. Sessions was coming around a corner

when Billy smacked into him. Since Billy's head was down, it put a dent into Mr. Session's stomach. Poor Mr. Sessions lost his breath and staggered. Holding to the wall he managed to keep from falling.

Billy froze. Gradually Mr. Sessions regained his composure and looked at Billy. "I'll see you in my office at one P.M." With as much dignity as possible Mr. Sessions marched to his quarters.

At lunch Billy wasn't hungry. He told the boys at his table about his coming "talk."

"Now if he offers to whip you, just take it," offered Ralph, a dark-haired, dark-skinned boy. "That's what I always do."

"I do too," explained Charles with his white, white hair and blue eyes. "I'd rather just get it over with."

"What else is there?" asked Billy.

"Well, he can make you walk the cinder path around the administration building. One time he made a boy walk the cinder path eight hours a day for a week. He only got time off to eat and sleep. No one was allowed to talk to him at all. Of course, that was for running away. That's the worst!"

"No, it's not! It's not at all!" chimed in several boys.

"What's the worst?" innocently inquired Billy.

"The worst is to talk to Mama Sessions."

They all agreed.

"That doesn't sound so bad," answered Billy.

"I saw her with the first-graders, and she seemed nice."

"Yeah, yeah—with the first-graders! But she talks to you the same way. She thinks everyone here is a first-grader," Ralph told him.

"Well, what does she do?" Billy couldn't see how a whipping could be better than talking to that sweet old lady.

"Oh, she cries. She begs you to be good. She tells you you are hurting Jesus. She prays! Oh, I don't know, but it is terrible—just terrible. She puts her hand on your chin and tips it up and says she loves you and weeps. When she does that to me I feel like dying right there on the spot. I'll take a whipping any day—any day," repeated Ralph.

Armed with this information, Billy approached the office at two minutes before one o'clock.

Mr. Sessions looked like he had recovered and wanted to talk. "I've been talking with your teachers and with the counselor on your ward. It seems they think you are neat and clean and you are doing very well except for two things. One is fighting and the other is running. What do you say for yourself?"

Billy couldn't think of anything to say for himself. He answered, "Nothing, sir."

"Well, I caught you running, so I'm going to punish you for that. Don't let me catch you fighting. Do you hear me?" ordered Mr. Sessions.

"Yes, sir!" answered Billy. He looked up into

Mr. Sessions's eyes, and they reminded him of Grandfather's eyes when he was stern. "I'll just take the whipping, sir, if you don't mind."

"Your punishment, Billy, is to run a mile every morning before breakfast. No matter what the weather. Well—if it is below zero degrees, you are excused. But every other day, rain or shine, run a mile every morning. Do it in the park. I can look out my window and see you every morning between seven and eight while I am dressing." If you are not there, we will have another talk. I'll put up markers so you will know how long the mile is. Do you understand?"

"Yes, sir!"

When Billy told the other boys, they all wanted to know how long he had to do it. "A week, a month—how long?" they asked.

"I don't know," answered Billy, "he didn't say." Billy never did know, so he ran every day until he left the orphanage.

Billy's first year at the orphanage taught him a lot of new games. He loved having enough children to play "Antney Over," "Crack the Whip," and "Bum Bum Bum, Here We Come!" But most of all he loved the baseball games. The orphanage had a team and played other schools. Billy was only thirteen, and all the boys on the first team were older. But they let him be on the practice team and soon found out that if he ever got on base he would steal his way home. He ran so fast no one could catch him.

Another thing Billy loved at the orphanage was

Halloween. All day the boys would sneak up behind people. They'd hit them with a sock full of
flour or mark up their clothes with chalk.

Also every boy made a tick-tack. He took an
empty wooden thread spool, cut notches in the
ends, and wrapped a string around the middle.
Then he put a stick through the spool so it had
something to spin on.

At night Billy would sneak up to somebody's
window. Then with one hand he would hold the
stick so that the spool pressed against the glass.
With the other hand Billy jerked the string. When
the spool started spinning against the glass it
made an awful noise. Billy loved to peek in the
window and see people jump out of their chairs.

Sometimes Billy and his friends would knock
on doors and then run. Those that were not fast
enough might get a dash of water in the face. But
Billy never did. He ran fast enough to escape.

Halloween was fun, but Billy also liked Easter.
For this one occasion the cook let them in the
kitchen. They formed a line and each boy picked
up three hard-boiled eggs. Billy dipped his first
egg in green water, made by boiling young blades
of wheat. The second egg he dipped in yellow
water made from the bark of a hickory tree. His
last egg he dyed brown in onion skin water.

Then on Easter Sunday Billy went about to his
best friends. "Want to knock?" he'd ask. When
Ralph said, "Sure," they each held up their eggs
with the small end pointing out. They knocked
the ends together. When Ralph's egg cracked,

Billy yelled, "Toc!" He was the winner. More important—he and Ralph were best friends. Since each boy had only three eggs, he wanted to be sure he played with his best friends.

The worst part of living in the orphanage in Glenwood in 1874 was not the dormitory, the classrooms, or the dining hall. It was the fighting.

Although the boys did fight among themselves, it was when the gang from West Side came to the orphanage playground that the trouble really began.

If the boys from the orphanage tried to ignore them they would yell:

> "Coward, coward,
> Buttermilk soured.
> Ain't been churned in
> Twenty-four hours!"

If Ralph would say he was going to tell a teacher, they'd call:

> "Tattletale,
> Tattletale,
> Hang your breeches
> On a nail."

One of the boys at the orphanage was very stout, and that was always a good thing to start a fight.

The West Side boys would yell:

> "Fatty, Fatty,
> Two by four

46

Swinging on the kitchen door.
When the door began to shake
Fatty had a tummy ache."

Then if the fat boy would run out with sticks to hit the gang, the fight was on. If not, the gang would keep on with something like:

"What's your name?
Hickory Ben Double.
Ask me again and
I'll give you trouble."

Soon the West Side gang found that they could always get the fight started by addressing Billy:

"Hee hee hee,
Can't catch me.
Can't catch a flea on
A Christmas tree."

Billy knew he could catch them, and he could stand there quietly only so long. Gradually the blood in his face boiled, and he would run out and catch the taunter. Once those two started, the whole crowd would be at it. The fighting didn't stop until a teacher or Mr. Sessions came out.

The authorities always punished the boy who fought first, so Billy ended up with many whippings.

7

Mother's Day Letter

"**M**r. Sessions says we have to have our Mother's Day letters ready to be mailed by breakfast time tomorrow."

Edward looked hard at Billy.

"Mr. Sessions says we are lucky to have a mother to write to. We had a whole hour to write letters after study period. Why didn't you get yours written?"

"I dunno. I guess I got to thinking about Ma and just didn't write."

"What were you thinking?"

"I just remembered how she always stood at the end of the lane when I was riding on the cow's back. Watch and I always brought the cows home from pasture, remember, Edward? Remember how she smiled so kinda sad and loving?"

"Yeah, and she is going to be sad if she doesn't get your letter for Mother's Day."

"I miss her, and I miss Watch, too. The orphanage is fine, and we get enough to eat and

49

don't have to work as hard as we did at home, but it's not the same. The teachers can't be mothers, leastwise not Ma."

"Billy, I know you miss home and I do too, but we have to go into the dining room for dinner now. After that we finish chores and study for two hours. When are you going to write Ma's letter?"

"I'd write in study hour, but you know how the monitors check to see your lessons, and I do have plenty of lessons. I'll just have to write after "lights out.""

"Now, Billy, how can you write without a light, I'd like to know."

"I'll put a candle under the covers," whispered Billy as they found their seats in the dining room.

Nearly dropping his tray of food, Edward whispered, "You'll burn down the whole place, that's what you'll do!"

"Well, what can I do?" Billy looked desperate.

"Eat your dinner and think of something."

During the study hour Billy managed to write a note to his brother and pass it under the table from student to student.

Edward stealthily opened it and read, "Sneak out to the watchman's gate."

Billy looked down the row of boys and saw Edward nod his head. He was glad he had a brother here. Once before they had slipped out to the watchman's gate to talk. The watchman had never reported them.

The worst part was to stay awake until all the

boys were asleep. Billy knew the beds were checked to see that everyone was safely sleeping before Annie lumbered off to her own bed.

While Billy was waiting he thought of Ma and Grandfather Corley. He recollected Grandfather's telling him, "Why, I remember when you were born—no bigger than your hand. We carried you around on a pillow for two years. That we did. You were so puny, boy!"

"But you're fine now," Ma interrupted. Billy remembered her shiny eyes and the little pat she gave him.

Grandfather, however, was full of his story. "Son, I don't know what would have become of you if it hadn't been for that doctor. He went out in the woods and gathered herbs and berries and roots and brewed a tea that just fixed you up in no time. He said you needed iron or something. That tea didn't look like iron, but it did the trick."

Billy remembered Ma's laughing. "Grandfather, you held your grandson on your hand, and Willie, you stood up on his hand straight as an arrow; both your little feet on his one hand. It was a sight. You weren't put in this world for nothing, not you. You wouldn't have lived through those first three years if God hadn't had a plan for you. No, sir-ee!"

With a start Billy came back to the present. He listened. All was quiet. Some boys were snoring, but nothing was moving. Billy felt the time had come to slip out of bed. He donned his pants and sweater and moved silently down the steps and outside. It was a clear, cool, spring night. There was Edward creeping along the bushes from his dormitory. Together they sped to the watchman's gatehouse and peeped in.

"Who's there?" a grumpy voice demanded.

"It's only us, Billy and Edward."

"I thought I told you I'd have to report you if you make a habit of slipping out of the dorm. Mind you, now what do you want?"

"We only need a little light to write a Mother's Day letter. It has to be done by breakfast time, Mr. Sessions says."

"Well, hurry it up, boys," commanded the watchman.

Billy brought out his crumpled paper and a dull pencil.

"What shall we write?" asked Billy.

"What do you mean *we?*" demanded Edward. "I already wrote mine. You write what you want to say to Ma."

Billy looked at the paper. He remembered Ma's reading to them. He remembered *Try and Trust,* the last book she had finished. He began to write.

> Dear Ma,
>   Here we try to be good. I try, too. I wish I could see you and Grandfather. How are you? I run a mile every day. It's good.
>   Love,
>   Billy

As Billy silently sneaked back to his bed he thought about his letter. He had not told Ma about the lump in his throat, the dryness of his tongue, and the ache in his heart. Grandfather said mothers were not for leaning on, but how he wished he could see her.

"I wish I could write a great letter to let Ma know how I feel. I wish I had a real talent for writing." Then Grandfather's words rang in his ears. "It's not the man of great natural talent who wins, but he who pushes his talent, however small, to its utmost capacity." *My letter is not important. It doesn't say how much I love Ma. Oh, well, it don't matter.*

He did not know that over fifty years later he would pull a piece of paper out of Mother's rusty, old trunk and find enough faded pencil marks to recognize it as his Mother's Day letter.

8

Welcome Home

Billy's second year at the orphanage was better. For one thing he was fourteen years old, and that put him in the senior group.

Now, when the West Side gang came to the playground fence Billy waited until someone else started the fight. Since the only one punished was the person who started the fight, Billy avoided being whipped.

He avoided demerits by keeping a neat room, pressing his clothes, and keeping his closet in order. In time, he grew to appreciate neatness. He also enjoyed Saturday afternoons in town, which were the reward for those with no demerits.

Another thing he really liked was being on the first team in baseball. That was the year the coach taught him how to bunt the ball. By bunting he could run to first base, and almost always he could steal his way home from there. He actually racked up more scores than boys who were good at hitting the ball. And scores win the games; everyone knew that.

Team by team, they beat their way up to the final city championship game. When they won that, Billy's heart felt like it would burst.

The teachers invited them over for fudge and hot chocolate. The principal gave a nice speech, pointing out all the good plays they had made. Although Billy received his share, no one ever suspected he would be a famous player one day.

Then the Chamber of Commerce had a luncheon and gave each boy a green and white sweater. Since Billy's was too large, he was still wearing it when he finished high school. At the time Billy felt that he could never ask for more from life.

All good things come to an end, however, and Mr. Sessions made an announcement the very next day. The whole orphanage was being moved to Davenport, Iowa. Other uses had been found for the buildings, and the city of Davenport had built a new, modern complex. All two hundred children would be moved. Billy realized he and Edward would move with them to Davenport.

School was much more difficult in Davenport. Billy found himself studying more diligently than he ever had before. He really intended to graduate from eighth grade. He had been told they had good baseball teams in high school.

Billy knew that when school was out Edward would leave the orphanage. No one stayed after he was sixteen. He wondered what would happen then.

Finally a day came when school was soon to be dismissed. The superintendent at Davenport, S. W. Pierce, sent for Edward Sunday to come to his office.

"Billy, go with me to see Mr. Pierce," Edward said. "You know I can't talk to people like that. I can't think of anything to say."

Billy laughed. "Well, I always wanted you to talk and you wouldn't so—now—I don't mind at all. I've had all the practice. Besides, I'm going with you wherever you go. I don't want to stay here alone."

"Alone! With six-hundred other students, how can you say you're alone?"

"Oh, you know what I mean!"

Mr. Pierce was very kind to the boys. "Your grandfather has answered our letter. He says he can use Edward on the farm since he is now old enough to look after himself."

"What about me?" demanded Billy.

"You are only fourteen, and you can stay here another two years." Mr. Pierce smiled.

"But I don't want to stay without Edward. We're brothers. We belong together. Please, Mr. Pierce, Grandfather always liked me. Let me go too!" pleaded Billy.

"Well now, your grandfather just said 'Edward,' " hesitated Mr. Pierce. "There isn't time for more letters, because we have arranged to put Edward on the train next Tuesday after graduation."

"Grandfather always petted me. He taught me

57

things. He will be tickled to see me and, oh, I would love to see him and my mother too." Billy could not help the sob that came into his voice.

Mr. Pierce was not a cruel man. "All right, Billy," he relented. "But you know you can't come back. That's the rule. Are you sure?"

"I'm sure," answered Billy.

In the morning hours of Tuesday, June 10, 1876, Billy marched in the graduation exercises. That same afternoon he boarded the train with Edward. They were headed for home in Ames, Iowa.

One look at Grandfather's face at the station made Billy realize he should not have come.

"You were not invited, Willie. You are not old enough to pull your weight around here, and no one is here to look after you. I'm an old man now and can't be annoyed with children anymore. Heigler has run off, and your mother is back home again with a new baby. We don't need any more trouble, Willie."

"But I'm not trouble, Grandfather. I'll do my part. See if I don't!" begged Billy.

Grandfather sniffed, and Billy was afraid to say any more as his mother took him in her arms.

Because there was nothing to do the next morning, Billy went over to the Agriculture College, where he used to play baseball with the college boys. He had been a great favorite with them when he was small.

The students Billy had known were all gone, but sure enough there was a game going on. One of the students called out, "You over there. Who are you, shrimp? Where did you come from?"

"I'm Squire Corley's grandson, Billy Sunday. I just came yesterday from Davenport. Can I play?"

"Is your grandfather the Squire Corley who gave this land to build the college?" quizzed another student, whose name was also Billy.

"Yes, that's the one."

"Well, yes, indeed—you may play, my boy. Take your place at the end of the batting line— right over there," said the first student.

Billy didn't like his tone of voice, but he went to the end of the line anyway.

When it was his turn to bat, the pitcher gave him an easy ball. Billy bunted it and scooted to first base before anyone was aware of what was happening. Billy led off first while the pitcher was warming up for his next throw. The pitcher saw him, however, and threw the ball to first. To his surprise Billy was back on first before the ball arrived. As soon as he started his pitch again Billy led off again. Three times the pitcher threw to first and three times Billy beat the ball.

The next pitch went to the batter, who knocked a short grounder and was put out on first. By this time Billy was safe on third base. He played the game of leading off on third until the college boys began kidding the pitcher, "What's the matter, Jack, the boy too fast for you?"

This unnerved the pitcher, and the next time

Billy led off, he threw the ball so fast and hard it went over the head of the third baseman. As this happened Billy ran home amid the cheers of his teammates.

There was no doubt about his welcome now. The college boys urged him to have lunch and stay for the afternoon games. He stayed until sundown, as a matter of fact.

That was what got him into trouble with Grandfather.

"Where have you been?" demanded Grandfather when Billy came into the house. "Look at the clock. Seven-thirty. What do you mean worrying us all day? What were you doing?"

"Why, I went over to the college to play ball. There wasn't anything to do here!" defended Billy.

"Yes, there was plenty of work here. You didn't look. Playing ball, were you! That beats the Dutch! Did you hear those fellows swearing?" asked Grandfather.

"Well, yes."

"And what did you do about it? Nothing, I see by your face. Don't you know that 'He who accepts evil without protecting against it is really cooperating with it' and 'If you lay down with dogs, you'll get up with fleas'? I won't have my grandson learning to drink and swear and gallivant around like those young ball players. If you don't want the fruits of sin, stay out of sin's orchard, I always say." Billy had never seen Grandfather like this. His face was red. The blood vessels under his eyes were puffed. Billy realized he must be sick or something.

Afterward he talked to his mother. "I can't stay here, I see," he said.

"No, Grandfather gets too upset. He will have a heart attack or a stroke. I'm so sorry, Willie. Let me try to think of something. Do you want to go back to the orphanage?" asked Mother.

"No, I can't do that!" was all Billy said.

In a few days Billy heard of a hotel in Nevada, Iowa, that was in need of an errand boy. That was something he could do. So when he found out one of the college boys was going the six miles to Nevada, he hitched a ride to apply for the job.

9

Nothing but Work

Though Nevada was only six miles from Ames, Billy had never been there before.

Early in July 1876 his student friend let him out of the buggy in front of the town's one hotel. "Now," he said, "before I go back I'll drive past here. If you are standing outside I'll pick you up. If not I'll assume you got the job. Good luck, little fellow!"

Billy took the bags and bundles of clothes he had brought from the orphanage. With beating heart he struggled up the steps and into the lobby, looking at the beautiful dark paneling, the fancy light fixtures, and the solid stone walls.

A hard-faced man with piercing black eyes and an enormous amount of black hair glared down at him from behind the counter. "Want a room?" he inquired.

"No. No, sir. I'm Billy Sunday. I heard you could use an errand boy here, and I came to get the job."

"I'm Mr. Boggs. Pleased to meet you."

Mr. Boggs took his time staring at Billy, not missing a single detail from the tattered shoes to the clear, steady, honest blue eyes.

"Well, now, what can you do, young man?"

"I can run errands and anything you want. What errands need to be done?"

"This isn't an easy job, and you are on duty all the time. I mean anytime we need you, we call, so you have to live here. Is that all right?"

"Oh, yes, sir, that is fine." Billy didn't say he had no where else to live.

"You look strong. I believe you might do, Billy Boy. Let me introduce you to my wife. She's the one you will have to please anyway."

Mrs. Boggs was more explicit about the duties and the pay. She took Billy into a side room to talk. Billy got the impression that she wanted a servant to do all the dirty jobs around the hotel—but then, he didn't have a place to stay, nor did he mind hard work. He was to get his meals, his room, and eight dollars a month. He took the job.

His room turned out to be the storage room in the basement. It was packed with dirty old furniture in need of repair. It really was only a place to store his clothes. He was to sleep behind a fake wall that contained a wall-bed, which he pulled out late at night. This hidden bed was located in the lobby behind the registration counter.

Each evening after dinner he watered and fed all the horses of the guests staying at the hotel. Then he came into the hotel and took a bath upstairs in the guests' beautiful hall bathroom. This he enjoyed after all his years of bathing in a wooden tub only on Saturday nights. Sometimes he would be outside on his way to the outhouse before he remembered that the hotel had inside plumbing.

After he changed clothes Billy would come down the long staircase to the registration counter where he welcomed guests, gave them keys to their rooms, and delivered mail. He stayed behind the desk until midnight. Then he was allowed to pull down the bed and sleep with his clothes on.

If someone wanted to check into the hotel after that, they rang a little bell, and Billy would stumble out and give them a room. Usually everyone was checked in by midnight. But some nights, like Saturday night, Billy didn't get too much sleep.

It didn't take long to find out that being on desk duty was the only easy part of the job. In the morning he watered and fed the horses before breakfast. After breakfast he helped with the dishes. They were hardly finished when Mrs. Boggs was ready to "do" the rooms. Every bed had to be changed unless the guests were staying over. Every carpet had to be swept with an oversized broom. Billy was surprised to find that sweeping carpet was a very hard job. At the orphanage they just dusted the wooden floors. That certainly was easier. After all the sweeping, they had to go back later and dust everything. Billy felt like he was spending his day chasing dust and dirt from one place to another.

By the time they finished, it was time for lunch and dishes again. Doing dishes for fifty to seventy people was no easy task.

In the afternoon the stables had to be cleaned. Shoveling manure wasn't fun either, but Billy remembered Grandfather's words "If you can't do what you like, like what you do."

Billy's favorite horses were Colonel John Scott's "grays." Billy wasn't required to curry the horses, but Colonel Scott's were being neglected, and Billy was sorry for them.

One day Colonel Scott came in and caught Billy just as he finished rubbing the horses and brushing their fur to make it shine.

"Well, now I know who has been caring for my beasts. They are beautiful, eh?"

"Oh, yes, sir." replied Billy. "I just love to keep them clean and shiny. They are the most beautiful horses I ever saw. I hope you stay at the hotel for a long time."

"I am staying until after Christmas. My wife is coming then, and we will be moving into our new house. Listen, I'll give you some extra money for taking extra care of my horses."

"Oh, no, I couldn't take it, sir. Mr. Boggs pays me, you know."

"Not much, I'll allow!" responded Colonel Scott.

Billy found out that Colonel Scott had once been Lieutenant Governor of Iowa. This made him like him even better. Colonel Scott never put on airs, but somehow you knew he was an important person.

The first day of the month was payday. Billy got his eight dollars in nice, new, crisp bills. When he got to his room he threw them up into the air as high as he could. He watched them all come floating down—drifting lazily to the floor. He felt wonderful.

Billy begged Mr. Boggs to let him go home to Ames for Christmas, but Mr. Boggs said, "Christmas! Are you crazy? That is our busy time. No, indeed, we will be needing you then."

"When can I go?" begged Billy.

"Well, I don't remember promising you any time to go off when I hired you. Do you?"

"No, but you know I want to see my mother and brother and even Grandfather. They are only six miles away, and it seems like a hundred."

"All right, all right! You can have twenty-four hours right after New Year's. The second of January will probably be a cold, quiet day in Nevada."

Christmas at the hotel was an exciting time. First they went to the woods and found a tree. It was a majestic tree. Billy was astonished to see how beautiful it looked in the hotel lobby. The top extended all the way to the paneled ceiling. Even without decorations it was a magnificent sight.

Billy spent all his free time at the desk, making colored paper chains for the tree. He strung endless chains of fluffy popcorn too. That really brightened up the dark green branches. Mrs. Boggs baked butter cookies and made a hole in each with a pin. Billy put a string through the hole, and when Mrs. Scott came, she helped hang them on the tree.

Mrs. Scott and Billy liked each other at once. He noticed that her arrangement of the decorations added an artist's touch. She also brought red apples and beautiful shiny oranges to put on the tree.

"How are you going to get them to hang on the branches?" Billy asked. "Are you going to put hooks in them?"

"Oh, Billy, I wouldn't bruise them that way. See this gauze? We'll make a little bag for each one and hang the bags from the tree branches. That way, we can pass out the fruit after the party."

By Christmas Eve everything was perfect. Colonel Scott surprised everyone by bringing in clip-on holders for candles.

Mrs. Scott and Billy climbed up and carefully placed a candle in each holder.

"Get a pail of sand and a pail of water," ordered Mr. Boggs. "You never know what will happen, and we are not going to burn the place down."

Billy obeyed. It was just a precaution.

It seemed everyone in town came to the hotel for the Christmas party. The men had filled bags with candy for the children—mostly hardtack in the shape of canes and ripples. The town orchestra came to play, and a lot of people wanted to dance. The hotel lobby was the only place large enough for dancing.

First, the Colonel and Mrs. Scott lit the candles. Everyone just stood and stared for five, ten minutes. They were filled with awe watching this beautiful, glowing, flickering tree. Then they blew out the candles, for it was too dangerous to let them burn very long.

Santa Claus came and passed out presents. Every child got a bag of candy. Besides that, Billy got a book from Mrs. Scott.

Billy did enjoy seeing Colonel and Mrs. Scott together. They seemed so happy. Billy hated to see them leave the hotel, but their new home was almost finished and Christmas about over.

When the second of January came, Billy started out very early to walk the six miles to Ames. Billy put on his green and white sweater under his coat. The wind was blowing, and it was very cold. The sky looked like a blizzard was in the making. He also put on his gloves and four-buckle overshoes over wool socks. He tramped along, whistling as he walked.

His visit was a great success. Grandfather was calm and received him warmly. He had been ill but was now feeling better. Edward was working the farm. Mother was keeping the house and tending to the new baby, who could now take a few steps. Before Billy knew it, darkness had descended and it was too late to start back that night.

Mother said, "Stay overnight, Billy. You can

go back in the morning. Mr. Boggs surely won't mind."

Mr. Boggs did mind, however. When Billy finally arrived after struggling the whole six miles through the snow and fighting the piercing cold wind, Mr. Boggs said, "You overstayed your twenty-four hours vacation, young man! You're fired!"

10

Stable Boy

When Mr. Boggs said, "You're fired!" Billy ran to the stable. He took a curry and brush and gave the "grays" a brushing such as they had never known.

He didn't want anyone to see his tears. If he worked fast enough he could choke down the lump that came from his heart to his throat.

Colonel Scott found Billy in the stable. "What's wrong?" he asked. If the colonel's eyes had not been so kind and loving, Billy could have answered.

Finally he could choke back his feelings enough to say, "I'm fired! I lost my job."

"Good," said Colonel Scott. "Now I can ask you something I've been wanting to say for months. Will you come to my new home and be my stable boy?"

"But Colonel Scott, I'm a failure!" Billy exploded. "I got fired from my job. Who wants a failure?"

Colonel Scott smiled. "If at first you don't succeed, you're running about average. You did your best to please Mr. and Mrs. Boggs. I saw how hard you were working. The only person who doesn't fail sometime is the one who doesn't try. Will you try again as my stable boy?"

"Oh, yes, sir!"

Colonel Scott extended his hand. It wasn't a handshake to Billy—it was a thank-shake.

Colonel Scott went into the hotel to talk to his wife. Mrs. Scott was angry. "That Mr. Boggs! It's all his fault. I believe he thinks business will be slow this winter and he can load all the work on his wife. A measly eight dollars a month! It was slavery—pure slavery!"

Colonel Scott smiled. "You may be right, but remember, 'A man can fail many times, but he isn't a failure until he begins to blame somebody else.' Billy is blaming himself for not getting back in twenty-four hours. Don't encourage him to blame someone else. He'll learn a lesson and be stronger for it. Let's go talk to him."

Holding hands, Colonel and Mrs. Scott found Billy down in the storage room packing his clothes.

Mrs. Scott rushed in and threw her arms around him. "Billy, welcome to our family. The colonel and I will be honored to have you in our new home. You know we are moving in this week. There is an extra bedroom down the hall from ours, and it will make a dandy boy's room. We do need to get things settled, though. You are going to high school. With your mind, it is a real crime for you to drop out of school."

"But, ma'am, what about the stable job?"

"You can do that early in the morning and after school."

"But, ma'am, I hardly have nice enough clothes for high school. My clothes from the orphanage are getting smaller every day."

"Your wages include room, board, and clothes," suddenly decided Mrs. Scott.

"And eight dollars a month!" added Colonel Scott.

"But that's more than I got at the hotel," objected Billy.

"This is a better job." Mrs. Scott laughed. "Really, we need you to make a family. The colonel and I always wanted a boy, and now I feel we have one. Is that all right with you, Billy?"

Billy could not speak. He just held out his arms, and the three of them hugged each other.

Mrs. Scott worked like a whirlwind. She decorated the spare room in red, white, and blue. She painted the chest to match the bed and found a red, white, and blue braided rug for the floor. Somewhere she found a desk and chair. She cut down several pairs of the colonel's old pants and also several shirts. Billy was very pleased with the pants. He could wear his green and white sweater over the homemade shirts.

At school, however, they ran into problems. Mrs. Scott insisted Billy start classes at once.

"But if he starts in the middle of the year, he

73

can't graduate with his class. He won't have enough credits. Besides, how can he do second-semester albegra without taking first-semester algebra?" demanded the principal.

"He can do everything except algebra and Latin. So let him take his algebra and Latin next year, and his government and history this year," pressed Mrs. Scott.

"It will be mixed up, Mrs. Scott, and when graduation time comes he may be disappointed, you know."

"We can worry about that four years from now," insisted Mrs. Scott.

"What do *you* want to do, Billy?" asked the principal.

"Well, I'd like to start now. The baseball season will start in a few months, you know."

"Oh! You like to play baseball, do you? We can use some help on the team—haven't had a winning streak for some time. Well, all right, Billy, but four years from now, remember I warned you about the missing credits."

After getting his books and working on the schedule, Billy finally got out of the principal's office. Mrs. Scott went home, and Billy was taken to his home room.

The first person he saw was Betsy. Her hair was so blonde it was almost white. She had deep brown eyes, and the twinkles were like the sun shining on a pond of water. Her face beamed at him as he took the only empty seat left in the room.

Miss Mills repeated, "Tell us your name, young man." And again, "Tell us your name, young man!"

Everyone the class snickered. They all noticed Billy's face and his complete deafness to the teacher. It was plain that Betsy's charms had struck again. Billy was to be her newest slave.

11

Pink Satin Slippers

"What's wrong with you, Billy?" inquired Mrs. Scott the next morning at breakfast. "You have never taken this long to feed and water the horses. Remember, you're on a tight schedule now. You don't want to be late for school."

"Yes ma'am," mumbled Billy. He spoke like a recording. Mrs. Scott realized this was the fourth "yes, ma'am" he had said this morning—nothing more.

"How do you like your new school books?" she tried again.

"Yes, ma'am," Billy answered with a vacant look.

"I believe you have gone to Jericho," muttered Mrs. Scott. When Billy spilled his milk and just let it drip over the table, Mrs. Scott exclaimed, "Billy Sunday! Pay attention to what you're doing! If you were old enough I'd think you were in love."

At that Billy's face turned crimson.

"You *are* in love! Oh, Billy—how could you be? It must be one of those high school girls you saw yesterday. I simply can't believe it. You are too young—too young."

Billy was only fifteen years old the winter of 1877, but he knew he wasn't too young to love Betsy—Betsy with the warm, loving eyes and beautiful long yellow-white curls.

Never had Billy seen anyone with dark brown eyes and lashes, finely arched brown eyebrows, and white hair. It was startling. He should not have been surprised when he overheard several boys talking.

"How did she make her hair white? I thought it looked beautiful when it was dark brown."

"She peroxides it. I heard if you soak your hair in peroxide it turns yellow or white."

"She sure must have soaked it a heap. That will show up when it start growing again. Nothing can make it *grow* out white like that."

Billy choked. *And to think I swallowed it, hook, line, and sinker,* he said to himself.

But when he caught a glimpse of Betsy down the hall and felt her love-filled eyes upon him he said to himself, *They couldn't be talking about Betsy. She takes the cake.*

He thought she took the cake at recess, too. She asked him, "Do you like riddles?"

"Oh, sure."

"Guess this one: What has eyes but cannot see?"

"A potato. I already heard that."

"What's the difference between a train and a teacher?"

"I dunno."

"A teacher says to throw away your chewing gum, and a train says, 'Choo-choo!' " Betsy laughed. "What fruit do you find on a dime?"

"I dunno."

"A date. What gets wetter the more it dries?"

"I dunno."

"A dishtowel, you goose," teased Betsy. She turned her brown eyes upward to Billy, and his heart turned completely over.

All afternoon he felt a glow of pure joy. Liquid tingles flowed through his veins. His toes vibrated. *How could anyone be so exciting?* Billy wondered. He learned a great deal that afternoon, but none of it came from his books.

Later in the day everyone was getting a drink of spring water from the wooden bucket. Each took a turn using the tin dipper. After Betsy had had a turn, she filled the dipper and offered it to Billy.

"Have a drink, Billy Boy."

"Why?" asked Billy.

"It will make you feel good, you goose!"

"But I already feel so wonderful," explained Billy, to Betsy's great amusement.

Billy didn't notice that the other students were even more amused. They knew Betsy's tricks.

Al, the last "new" boy in town spoke privately to Billy. "Listen, I fell for all that stuff just like you are doing. It ain't worth it. Believe me!"

"What stuff you talking about?" asked Billy.

"Betsy's stuff. You think we can't see you're lovesick?"

Billy felt foolish. "I didn't think anyone would know."

"Don't feel bad. Every new boy that comes to the high school gets the treatment. Then they find out about Herbert."

"Who's Herbert?"

"Herbert is the best-looking senior in high school. He's captain of the baseball team and a real ladies' man. He's courting Betsy, even though she is only a freshman. I even heard they go down by the river and spoon."

"Spoon?"

"Yes, kiss and that stuff."

"But when she looks at me—she is so pretty."

"Yeah, I know, I know." Al sighed as he walked into his algebra classroom.

A few weeks after Billy started high school there was a Valentine's party in the lunchroom. Billy was glad it was after February first because he now had his eight-dollar salary. With eight dollars he knew he could bid for Betsy as his lunch partner.

The girls would all stand behind sheets so that only their shoes could be seen. The auctioneer would ask for bids on each pair of shoes, and the highest bidder got to eat lunch with the girl who was wearing those shoes. Billy was looking forward to eating lunch with the prettiest girl in the school.

At last it was lunchtime. Billy knew it would be easy to pick Betsy's shoes because they were the only pink satin shoes in the room. There they were, peeking out from under the sheet, the third pair down the line.

Billy was ready when the bidding started. Al started it out with 50 cents. Every time someone added 50 cents Billy would bring it up to another dollar. Herbert gave a loud $7.50, and Billy knew it was his last chance. "Eight dollars!" he called as the crowd gasped. Usually no bid was over $3.00 or $4.00. Billy was determined.

"Sold. Sold to the gentleman for eight dollars," he heard the auctioneer call out loudly. He heard thunderous clapping. In a daze he gave up his eight crisp bills. He saw the pink satin slippers move out from behind the sheet. Only Betsy was not wearing them! Everyone in the room roared. The girls had exchanged shoes.

Red-faced, Billy took Emaline Berglesteed by the hand and led her over to the lunch counter.

12

High School Days

The winter of 1879, when Billy was a junior, he looked back at his first two years of high school with amusement.

Now that he could see through Betsy, it was difficult to believe he had been one of her captives. He remembered Mrs. Scott's repeating, "Pretty is as pretty does." Betsy didn't seem pretty to him anymore.

Some of the things he had done with the fellows were not so pretty either. He remembered upsetting outhouses on Halloween. Once they had put old man Brickly's buggy on the roof of the courthouse. *That wasn't easy—or kind,* he reflected.

Billy remembered warm Sunday mornings. He and his friends would amuse themselves while walking to church. The farmhands came to town Saturday nights, got drunk, and lay asleep on the board sidewalk. The boys would get a running start and leap over their bodies, letting out piercing screams. Afterward they always looked back to see the startled look on the men's faces. Wherever Billy went, excitement followed.

Sometimes the excitement wasn't welcome. He remembered last winter, when he was a sophomore. At recess the boys all threw snowballs at the town clock on the Methodist Church across the street from the high school. They tried to get enough snowballs to stick on the clock to stop the hands.

When a teacher saw them he ordered them inside the schoolhouse and proceeded to lecture. "You boys throwing snowballs at the Lord's building—dreadful—dreadful!" he said.

He kept looking at Billy, although Billy had not thrown any more snowballs than the others.

Finally Billy could keep quiet no longer. "I wasn't throwin' 'em at the Lord's building. I was throwing' 'em at the town clock."

Down the aisle came the teacher. Billy went under the seat, but the teacher grabbed him, tore his shirt—and let him have it, as he told Mrs. Scott later.

Mrs. Scott pointed out that if he had not been doing something he shouldn't, nothing would have happened. "Billy, you are going to have to learn to keep quiet. Just don't open your mouth." Those words stuck in Billy's mind and saved him on many many occasions later in life.

At first Billy's job at the stable kept him so busy he didn't have time to hang around the drugstore with the other fellows. Gradually, however, Billy increased his speed to the point that he could finish his work and still get down to the drugstore before the fellows left. They stood out front, fooled around, made a racket, blocked the door, and in general aggravated the owners. When they tired of that they stood under the streetlight and threw pebbles.

Another time Billy remembered well was the Fourth of July in Nevada. First there was a parade, then races. Billy always won something. In the afternoon they had a ballgame with a team from another town. It was soon evident that Billy helped the team win by making scores—mostly by stealing bases. At night there was a dance, but Billy was more interested in the fireworks. They had firecrackers called "Baby Walkers" and "Torpedoes." Also they had big cannon crackers they put under hats. When the firecrackers went off, the hats were blown to bits. But it wasn't fun when one youngster lost a hand and another several fingers.

Billy's junior year was different. He felt like putting away childish things. For one thing he was seventeen, almost eighteen years old, and for another he had a responsibility.

He was responsible for the janitorial work at the high school. On Monday mornings he was at the school by 3:00 A.M. He kept old newspapers handy and had a collection of shavings. He whittled many pieces of wood so that thin wooden strips curled lazily down two sides. These he arranged over the newspapers and carefully lit the paper. As soon as this was burning and the wooden curls catching fire he added heavier and heavier wood and finally the coal. If this was done correctly the fire could last all week with only periodic additions of fuel and banking at night. Also he had to clean away the ashes, sweep the floors, and dust the classrooms.

It all seemed worthwhile when he got his $25.00 check each month. He was sometimes more faithful to his jobs than he was to his books. Mrs. Scott more than once found him sleeping over his homework.

The schoolboard said, "We have never seen so much coal used before." But the students said, "We have never been so warm before." And the board was faithful with his check. Billy was proud to see his name there. He took the check to the Farmers' Bank to cash.

One day at the end of April Billy took his check as usual to the Farmer's Bank. As usual he stood in line watching others cash their checks. When his turn came he spoke politely to Jay King as he shoved the check under the grating. Out came several bills, and Billy walked away smiling at the cashier.

When he counted his money later, however, he found that he had not $25.00 but $40.00.

Billy's first thought was to take the extra $15.00 back to the bank. On his way he met a lawyer friend of the colonel's.

Billy inquired, "Frank, what do you think? Jay

King handed me forty dollars, and my check only called for twenty-five dollars."

The lawyer said, "Bill, if I had your luck I would buy a lottery ticket."

"But the fifteen dollars is not mine!"

"Don't be a chump. If you were shy ten dollars and you went back you would not get it. If they hand out fifteen dollars, don't be a fool. Keep it!"

Billy went on down the street. He spied a brown suit with little green flecks in a window, and he walked into the general store. After checking the size, he asked the price. Fifteen dollars was exactly what he had.

"I'll take it," he said. It was his first suit of store clothes, and as he said afterward, "I thought I was the goods!"

Many years later Billy Sunday told an audience of thousands of people the rest of the story:

Years afterward when I said, "I ought to be Christian," and I got on my knees to pray, the Lord seemed to touch me on the back and say: "Bill, you owe that Farmers' Bank fifteen dollars with interest." I said, "Lord, the bank don't know that I got that fifteen dollars," and the Lord said, "*I* know it."

So I struggled along for years, probably like some of you, trying to be decent and honest and right some wrong that was in my life, and every time I got down to pray, the Lord would say: "Fifteen dollars with interest, Nevada County, Iowa. Fifteen dollars, Bill."

Years afterward I sent that money back, enclosed a check, wrote a letter, and acknowledged it. I have the peace of God from that day to this, and I have never swindled anyone out of a dollar.

13

Graduation Day Choice

"**B**illy, what are you going to wear for graduation?" inquired Mrs. Scott.

"My brown suit with the green flecks, I suppose—if I go."

"What do you mean 'if you go'? You know you are going to your graduation from high school," protested Mrs. Scott.

"You know it's a fake graduation for me, Mrs. Scott. I don't have enough credits to graduate. You know I lack two credits, and my diploma will not be signed when I walk across the platform to pick it up. The whole thing is false for me, and I really don't even want to go."

"Now, Billy, don't feel that way. You can finish those two credits next fall and get your diploma signed in January. Be a good boy and go to the graduation."

Mrs. Scott did not realize how Billy would feel next fall without one of his class members in school. He wouldn't be a senior. He wouldn't be anything.

Billy closed his lips and said nothing. Later he went out to the stable to think. He could always think better when his hands were busy.

He had a problem he had not explained to dear Mrs. Scott. The captain of the fire brigade in Marshalltown, Iowa, had visited Billy while he was doing his janitorial work at the high school.

They had talked a long time. "What we need is fast man to win the tournament on Friday." Friday was graduation day in Nevada. "We are offering you a job on the fire brigade. You can stay at the fire station and answer calls when there is a fire at night. This won't take all your time, so you can get another job during the day.

"We really need you to be our man at the races. Everyone says you can run faster than anyone else. We heard you have won the Fourth of July races for several years. If you could win the race for our team and help in the baseball game, you could put our team on the top of the tournament. How about it?"

Billy wasn't worried about winning the race. He was worried about Mrs. Scott. She would be so disappointed if he didn't graduate. But the job as a fireman was very desirable. It wouldn't be open in January, and the fire brigade really did need him right away.

As he cleaned the stable he resolved to go to Marshalltown. He dreaded telling Colonel and Mrs. Scott. They had been wonderful to him, and he didn't want to seem ungrateful.

After work Thursday night, he knew he could delay telling them no longer. When he came into the house he looked at the Scotts reading together.

"Colonel, I have to tell you and Mrs. Scott something," he stated.

"Yes, Billy, what is it?" kindly inquired the colonel.

"I'm going to Marshalltown to be a fireman tomorrow."

"What!" cried Mrs. Scott. "You can't do that!"

"Yes, I can. The captain of the fire brigade came and asked me. They're having a tournament tomorrow and need a fast man on their baseball team."

As Mrs. Scott's face flushed and she looked as though she would explode, the colonel patted her arm and said, "Dear, dear! Listen! Billy is nineteen years old. He can do what he thinks is best. The fireman's job is well considered, so don't try to stop him." The colonel looked kind but stern, and Mrs. Scott shut her eyes to hide the tears. She didn't protest further.

In fact she flew into a whirlwind of activity. She washed every piece of Billy's clothing. She laid his green and white sweater on papers, stretching it to the proper size so it would dry nicely. She even washed his brown suit in gasoline and hung it outside to dry and "air" overnight. In the morning she pressed it so that when it was time to catch the train Billy was scrubbed, cleaned, and felt like he had a new lease on life.

When Billy said, "good-bye," his heart was heavy with gratitude and love for these dear folks. He knew he was now "on his own," but he felt he was ready. He remembered Grandfather's saying, "It is not the man of great natural talent who wins, but he who pushes his talent, however small, to its utmost capacity."

Billy Sunday felt ready to push!

In Marshalltown the tournament went well. Billy enjoyed the crowds and the cheering for the various brigades.

Marshalltown won second place for the speed of their men in donning the fire-fighting outfits. Billy watched as they flung the long-sleeved heavy tunics around their bodies and buckled the awkward fabric clasps. He saw them sling the lanterns over their shoulders and fasten the straps. Then he watched as they put the stocking-like caps over their heads and adjusted the masks with the huge holes through which their eyes peered. Each cap fit down over the neck and had to be buttoned to the tunic. It was easy to see this action slowed up the men. They made up the time by jumping into the large black books and slipping their hands into the heavy gloves. At that moment they grasped the hose and pretended to be putting out a fire. The timekeeper pressed his stopwatch and recorded the speed of the whole operation. Billy tried to imagine himself dressing that quickly.

Next they had a competition to see which brigade could pump the most water in five minutes. Three strong men stood on each side of the "county fire office," as their fire engines were called. A bar extended down each side, and together the men moved the bar up and down to pump the water. They let Billy hold the hose over the trough, which was marked by 5-gallon lines. He was so excited when Marshalltown was ahead he almost dropped the hose. In the end Marshalltown came in second.

Just before the picnic, the races were held. The first was the 100-yard dash. By running the 100 yards in ten seconds Billy left everyone else in the dust. The audience gasped. "Who is that?" The name *Billy Sunday* was stamped on everyone's mind that day, and the Marshalltown Fire Brigade added points to their total. It was apparent that the final winner would be determined by the baseball game to be played after the picnic.

It was soon obvious that Marshalltown's new member was also a good baseball player. Billy used his bunt the first pitch he got and sped to first base so quickly the other team was still blinking. Then he began stealing bases and was home in no time. Soon the score was 3 to 0. All three scores resulted from Billy's base stealing. The audience howled, and the Marshalltown Brigade captain saw how wise he had been to enlist Billy for his team.

After the tournament, everyone in Marshalltown knew who Billy Sunday was. Billy felt very strange walking down the street and hearing all the new people call him by name, ask to shake his hand, and thank him for "putting Marshalltown on the map," as they said. Even Charles H. Hall, mayor of Nevada, met him one day and greeted him like an old buddy. "We knew you had it in you," he said. "That's the boy, Billy! You showed 'em, didn't you?"

Although Billy had a place to sleep in Marshalltown, the fire brigade did not pay a regular salary and there were no meals furnished. He quickly found that he did need another job to support himself.

Since Marshalltown was not a large city in 1880, Billy looked down Main Street and decided to go into every store and ask for a job—any job. To his inquiry he was told, "No. No, we don't need any help."

He had come to the last store and felt that there was no need to be told no again. This was a furniture store, and he knew he was ignorant about furniture. *Still, they could need a delivery boy. What do I have to lose by asking?* Billy asked himself.

He pulled up the pants to his brown suit, adjusted the jacket with the green flecks, and marched into the store.

The owner, Mr. Willard, looked at him. "Aren't you the young fellow who was in the fire brigade tournament?"

"Yes, and you know the fire brigade doesn't

pay a salary, so I really do need a job. I'm used to working. I've been a stable boy and a janitor at the high school."

"Was your work satisfactory, young man?"

"Yes, sir."

"You were dependable and easy to learn?"

"Oh, yes, sir!"

"Are you squeamish?"

"No, what do you mean?" inquired Billy.

"Have you been around dead people?"

"Well, no. Why?"

"I need an assistant at my mortuary and someone to help when we have funerals," explained Mr. Willard.

"But this is a furniture store," protested Billy.

"I know. I need help here delivering furniture and showing customers around. But I also need an assistant at the mortuary. I pay three dollars a week. If there is a fire, I'd excuse you to go with the brigade, and I'd also let you off to practice and play on the baseball team. I can see they need a man with your speed. How about it? You want the job?"

Billy felt doubtful, but he had asked everywhere else in town. If this was the only job open, he decided he had better take it. His whole future might hang on his decision.

"I'll take the job, Mr. Willlard," he said.

14

The State Championship Game

The next three years of Billy's life taught him many things. He learned to sell furniture. If he could get the customers to see themselves and their families living with the furniture, they would buy it. Thus, he became very proficient at painting word-pictures for the customers.

Billy also learned to comfort those who had lost loved ones. At first this was difficult. Then he remembered Grandmother and how his heart was broken when she died. He still hurt when he remembered her saying, "It takes both rain and sunshine to make a rainbow."

There was a difference in death, Billy learned. When a Christian died there was comfort. When a non-Christian died, there was no comfort. For the next three years Billy ushered at almost every funeral in Marshalltown. He felt he never wanted to hear another funeral sermon—never.

Billy also learned about fighting fires. He saw the firemen risk their lives. The "office" was slow getting to fires because the men had to push and pull it. He heard that some large cities had horse-drawn carts. Some even discussed getting modern equipment for Marshalltown, but there was never enough money. They were lucky to have so few fires in Marshalltown. Sometimes Billy felt they just went to the fires to keep people under control and to rescue those inside burning buildings. If the fire was well started when they arrived, there was really little they could do.

Billy also learned to be adaptable on his various jobs. One minute he would be racing to a fire, the next hour would find him selling furniture, and late afternoon would see him comforting an old lady who had lost her husband. Billy did whatever needed to be done. He never dreamed that every experience was planned by God to prepare him for the Lord's work.

Actually there was more talk around the fire station about the state championship baseball games than about fires. The Marshalltown team had practiced faithfully. They knew each other's strengths and weaknesses. They knew they could count on Billy to steal bases and make scores if he ever got on first base. Soon every rival team also knew he could only bunt the ball. They all crowded up to him when he was batting. They could get the ball as soon as it left his bat and catch him before he could start running. If he was too fast for them, however, he would soon be on first base. Everyone said, "If Billy could only hit the ball, what a great player he'd be."

Even with this drawback, however, the team had victories over five of the rival teams. Billy was elated. "This is the best chance we ever had. Come on, gang, let's do it. Why shouldn't we be state champions in 1883? We've got the best team in the state of Iowa."

Game by game they worked their way up. Soon they really were in the running. "The team that believes it can win is probably right, and so is the team that believes it can't," their coach said. "How many of you believe we can be the state champions? If you believe it, we can! Don't forget that!"

Billy was filled with enthusiasm. He checked carefully and could not find another team as good. He talked to every discouraged teammate and overcame all doubts. Soon everything clicked. They won and they won and they won again. Finally the day came when they really were to play in the championship game.

It so happened the game was to be played in Marshalltown. There was a rumor that "Pop" Anson, manager of the Chicago White Stockings, might be there.* Pop Anson was a brother-in-law to Mr. Willard and was coming to visit his sister that very weekend.

The day of the game was hot and sunny, usual Iowa weather in the summer. Each team member had acquired enough money to buy his own uniform. After Billy had topped all sales records selling furniture, Mr. Willard gave him a bonus. It

*The Chicago White Stockings later became the Chicago Cubs.

was enough money for his uniform. Billy wore this uniform with pride. He told his teammates, "We look like the goods in these outfits. Now let's play that way."

"Play ball!" the umpire shouted as the championship game started. Billy always led the batting order because everyone knew if he ever got on first base, he was almost sure to make a score. He knew everyone was aware of his bunt, and sure enough all the players rushed up toward home base. Billy fooled them and batted a weak fly. It could have been easily caught, but the fielder had gone over to first base, thinking he would put Billy out there. The ball bounced helplessly in the field, and Billy was on second base before the fielders could get back into position. He stole to third almost at once and was home as soon as one of his teammates batted a grounder. Marshalltown led the scoring from the very beginning and easily won. Every time Billy's turn came, he scored. The crowd cheered and howled.

Pop Anson was in the crowd. He was immediately impressed with Billy's playing.

After the game Mr Willard sought out Billy and introduced them.

Pop Anson said, "Your speed would be an asset to any team, young man."

"Oh, Mr. Anson, do you suppose I could ever play with the Chicago White Stockings? Could I hope to be good enough for the big leagues?"

"Young man, I don't often encourage local players with as little experience as you have, but let me think about this. I'll talk it over with the owner of our team, Mr. Spaulding, and I'll send for you to try out next spring. I'm not promising you anything, you understand, but a tryout. I believe your speed deserves that!"

Billy was elated by the promise. It was a promise Pop Anson kept, and the spring day came when Billy Sunday boarded the train at Marshalltown and rode into Chicago and a new life.

Billy noticed a tall, strong, athletic-looking young man at the front of the coach. He wondered if it was his imagination that the porter seemed to favor the young man, bringing him a magazine to read and even a drink of water. Other passengers nudged each other and looked several times at the young man. Billy wondered who he was.

When the train arrived in Chicago, Billy was surprised to see so many people at the station. Crowds and crowds of people hurried past him as though he didn't exist. Never had Billy imagined so many people in one place. If Pop Anson had not found him, he would have wandered aimlessly for hours. To his surprise, Pop Anson was accompanied by the young man who had sat at the front of the coach during Billy's entire trip.

"Mike Kelly, meet Billy Sunday. This is the young man I was telling you about!"

Mike Kelly and Billy smiled and shook hands, while Pop Anson explained. "Kelly is the undefeated runner on our team. I wrote and told him

101

I'd bet ten dollars you could beat him in a foot race."

"And I took you up on the bet," Mike laughed.

The three of them took their luggage and walked toward the subway station. Billy was dazed by the tall buildings, the rattling overhead trains, and the clanging trolley cars. Never had he seen such an abundance of signs—some even flashing with lights. Billy had heard that electric lights were taking the place of gas lights in Chicago, but he was not prepared for the blaze and excitement of the city.

But he was prepared to run a race anytime, anywhere. So he dared Mike Kelly to settle the bet.

Kelly turned to Sunday. "'Strip your linen," he said.

Billy peeled off as many clothes as the law allowed and prepared to run. Anson marked out 100 yards on the main boulevard.

Kelly scoffed, "I can beat you with my coat on, country boy!"

Down the street they sprinted to the amusement of onlookers. For some time they ran side by side and neck to neck. Then Sunday pulled away and left Kelly to eat the dust from his heels.

Billy never knew whether that was his tryout, or if the games he played with the team later were the tryout. Somehow it became an accepted fact that he was on the team.

When Anson presented him with a contract to play with the Chicago White Stockings for the year 1883, Billy signed with glee. Imagine getting $60 a month for playing ball when he had been working for $3 a week and playing ball for nothing.

It was too good to be true!

15

The Big Leagues

Billy soon found that the big league played a different brand of baseball from that of firemen of Iowa.

They pitched balls so fast Billy hardly had time to position his bat. When he did connect, his bat went backward with the ball instead of directing the ball anywhere.

Because Billy had speed and could steal bases he was put at the front of the line-up of batters and therefore started many games. He approached the plate with a little fear. He'd miss one or two pitches, hit a foul ball, and strike out. He made sixteen outs for the Chicago "White Sox." During all this time, he never got on first base. He thought he heard a sneer as he approached the plate the seventeenth time in his career as a big league player. He resolved to get a hit this time.

"Strike," he heard the umpire call. He hardly knew the pitch was coming before it was over the plate. "Strike," called the umpire as the second pitch sailed over the left corner of the plate. Billy determined to hit the next one. He swung wildly at the next pitch, which was way out, and heard "strike three" called. After seventeen outs he walked away dejected. Why had he ever thought he was a baseball player? This league was just too fast for him.

Because he was so bad at the plate, he tried fielding to make up for it. He did prove that he could catch the ball. Because his fast legs could speed to the point where a fly was coming down, he made many "outs" for the team. His judgment concerning speed and direction was superior. If he could only bat the ball, he'd be happy.

His eighteenth time up to bat he got a bunt. Off he shot to first base and was pronounced "safe." He stole second, and to the other players' surprise he stole third. The next batter hit a home run, and both players came home. Those two scores won the game. After that the other players treated Billy with a little more respect.

But at the end of the first season Billy came home to Marshalltown completely disgusted with himself. He told Mr. Willard, "I hope I can have my old job back. I'll never get a contract for another year. I have got to hit the ball, or I will never be a big league baseball player."

Mr. Willard encouraged him. "Billy, you are only exempt from failures if you make no effort. Remember what happens around us is largely out of our control, but how we react to it is inside our control."

"You're right. I'm going to learn to bat that ball or die. I promise!" Billy practiced batting every day. Batting—batting—batting. At night he even dreamed of batting the ball.

In Chicago, Mike Kelly still had faith in Billy Sunday. Since Mike was captain of the team his recommendation was honored, and Billy was finally offered a contract for another year.

The night Billy left on the train he told his friends, "Watch me connect." This time he knew what big league baseball was all about. He knew of the speed and cleverness of all the other players. Most important, he had finally learned to bat the ball.

Billy Sunday was so good that year he topped the batting list on the Chicago team. From then on he was a valued member of the White Stockings. The fans loved him and often called to him as he was playing. His "smart" retorts filled them with glee and endeared him to the hearts of the crowd. Billy Sunday was loved by thousands, and his name became a household word. Life was simply one baseball game after another. For four years he gloried in his fame.

One day Billy was surprised to get a letter from Squire Corley. The writing was very shaky. "Son," began Grandfather, "you are famous now and think you are the goods, but fame doesn't bring peace to the heart. I fancy you are doing things with the baseball boys that would break your mother's heart if she knew. You may think you are on top of the world, but count the cost. Is it worth it?"

Billy was frankly surprised. He had always wanted to be a credit to Squire Corley. He had hoped that being a famous person would please the old gentleman. When he complained to his mother she wrote: "Willie, we are never more discontented with others than when we are discontented with ourselves. Examine yourself, boy, what is making you discontented with yourself? Grandfather has not changed his values. Have you?"

Billy did look at himself. He was doing everything the other players did to have fun. He went to the taverns, drank strong drink, teased the cheap girls, tried to smoke cigars, wore flashy clothes, and copied the vulgar language of the other players. *I'm only having fun,* he told himself. *I've worked hard to get where I am. I deserve to have a good time. I want to be one of the fellows.*

One of the books the fellows were discussing in 1886 was Jules Verne's new book *Journey to the Center of the Earth.* It told of great dreams of the future. It talked about submarines that could run under the sea. How the baseball players laughed. "No one could ever stay in the submarines. They would die for lack of oxygen!"

The book also told of planes that could fly in the air. "How ridiculous! Everyone knows nothing heavier than a bird could stay in the air." The players laughed.

Most impossible of all, the book told of sending pictures through the air from city to city. This idea brought down the house. Everyone was sure such a thing could never happen. The team was united and felt a good spirit of agreement.

Some strange things were happening, however. Billy bought a coffeepot one day that could be plugged in to the electricity and would heat water and make coffee. It was a great thing to have in the locker room on cold days. And the baseball office housed a new typewriter that printed when you pressed the right keys. Billy had searched out the keys and printed his name. They also had a cash register that speeded up the sale of tickets to the games and kept a record of the sales. It was like a miracle, Billy thought.

One of the players came into the locker room one day with a cigar lighter. Everyone had to try it out, whether he smoked or not. Billy said, "It beats the Dutch! It sure does! I wonder what they will think of next!"

Billy enjoyed going places with the other ball players, and Chicago was noted for its many saloons. One evening Billy went with the players to a saloon and drank with the boys. They wandered down Van Buren Street and sat down on the curb of a vacant lot.

A company of men and women from the Pacific Garden Mission was holding a street service.

They were singing gospel hymns, the same gospel hymns that Billy's mother sang back in the log cabin in Iowa.

Later Billy told of this day. "God painted on the canvas of my memory a visual picture of the scenes of other days and other faces. I sobbed and sobbed, and a young man stepped out and said, 'We are going down to the Pacific Garden Mission. Won't you come down to the mission? You can hear drunkards tell how they have been saved and girls tell how they have been saved from the red light district.' I rose and said to the boys, 'I'm through. I'm going to Jesus Christ!' Billy left his friends sitting on the curb and went to the mission with the singing group.

That night when Billy Sunday got home, he began to think of the laugh the gang would give him the next morning at practice. He could not sleep. He wasn't sorry he had gone to the mission, but he knew that he would have to face the gang.

Years later Billy Sunday told thousands of listeners what happened that day.

> The first to meet me was Mike Kelly. "Bill, I'm proud of you. Religion is not my long suit, but I'll help you all I can," he said. Then up came the rest. There wasn't a fellow in that gang who knocked me: every fellow had a word of encouragement.
>
> That afternoon we played the old Detroit club. We were neck and neck for the championship. I was playing right field, and John G. Clarkson was pitching.
>
> We had two men out, and they had a man on second

110

and one on third and Bennett, their catcher, was at bat. Charley had three balls and two strikes on him. Charley couldn't hit a high ball, but he could kill them when they were about his knee.

I hollered to Clarkson and said, "One more and we got 'em."

You know every pitcher digs a hole in the ground where he puts his foot when he is pitching. John stuck his foot in the hole and he went clear to the ground. Oh, he could make them dance. He could throw overhanded, and the ball would go down and up like that. That ball would go by so fast that a thermometer would drop two degrees. John went clear down, and as he went to throw the ball his right foot slipped and the ball went low instead of high. I saw Charley swing hard and heard the bat hit the ball on the nose. I saw the ball rise in the air and knew it was going clear over my head. I could judge within ten feet of where the ball would light. I turned my back to the ball and ran.

The field was crowded with people, and I yelled: "Stand back!" And the crowd opened like the Red Sea opened for the rod of Moses. I ran on, and as I ran I made a prayer; it wasn't theological either, I tell you that. I said, "God, if You ever helped mortal man, help me get that ball, and You haven't very much time to make up Your mind, either."

I ran and jumped over the bench and stopped. I thought I was close enough to catch it. I looked back and saw it going over my head. I jumped and shoved my left hand out, and the ball hit it and stuck. At the rate I was going, the momentum carried me on and I fell under the feet of a team of horses. I jumped up with the ball in my hand.

We won the game.

16

Changes

Billy Sunday did not stop with one visit to the Pacific Garden Mission. He went again and again. He saw men and women who had gone to the depths of sin ask Jesus to forgive them. Sunday saw their changed lives and listened to their testimonies of gratitude and faith.

He remembered the day he had almost drowned in Squaw Creek. Someone had reached down and saved his life. Now he wanted someone to reach down and save his soul. Billy Sunday asked Mrs. Clark, wife of the founder of the Mission, to help him. She read John 3:16: "For God so loved the world, that he gave his only begotten Son, that whosoever believeth in Him should not perish, but have everlasting life."

"Do you believe Christ died for your sins?" asked Mrs. Clark.

"Yes, I do," responded Billy.

"Why don't you tell Him you believe in Him and ask Him to save your soul?"

"I will," said Billy. He bowed his head and said, "Jesus, I believe You died for my sins. Come in and save this sinner."

"Did He come in?" asked Mrs. Clark.

"Yes!"

"Then you have everlasting life, Billy." And Mrs. Clark quoted John 3:16 again.

Billy Sunday was happy. He told Mrs. Clark about the day he almost drowned. Then he told her about his mother's prayers. "Mother always said I was saved for a reason. Now I know what it is—to serve Jesus."

But Billy Sunday was a baseball player. He had a contract with the White Stockings. He had promised certain things.

One thing he had promised was a footrace with Artie Latham, the fastest man in the American League in 1887. Everyone knew that Billy was the fastest man in the National League. The race had been arranged for months.

For months the baseball players had been putting all the money they could spare into a bet on Billy Sunday. The problem was that the race was on Sunday afternoon, and Billy would have to go to St. Louis. He had learned in Sunday school, "Remember the Sabbath day to keep it holy." How could he run a race, encourage men to gamble, and still keep Sunday holy?

Because Billy could not answer the question himself, he went to Pop Anson and said, "Pop, I can't run that race on Sunday."

Pop said, "Bill, don't show the white feather.

We've got twelve thousand dollars bet on you, and all the boys have bet their last cent on you. If you don't win that race they'll have to eat snowballs next winter. You go down to Saint Louis and run."

At the time Billy felt he should follow Pop's advice. He ran the race and beat Artie Latham by fifteen feet. But on Monday he went to Mr. Spaulding and Pop Anson. He explained that he could not play ball on Sunday anymore. He knew they could tell him he had broken his contract and was out of a job. But they agreed that his services on six days a week were too valuable to insist on Sunday games. Billy Sunday never played another ball game or ran another race on the Lord's Day.

Sundays were now spent in attending church services. Soon people recognized the ball player and were asking him to give his testimony about salvation. Public speaking was never Billy's strong point, but when he started telling about Jesus he forgot about himself. People always paid close attention to everything he said.

He began getting invitations from churches to speak to boys' Sunday school classes. The boys had seen him play ball. Every member of the class would come and bring a friend if Billy Sunday was speaking.

One Sunday morning after such a meeting, a small boy approached Billy and asked him to stay for church.

"Please stay and sit by me," begged George

Thompson. "Everyone will think I'm the goods if you sit by me."

Billy was amused and walked in and sat near the front as directed. The church interested him. He had never been in a Presbyterian church before and liked the quiet elegance, the quiet people, and the quiet, reverent service. It was a change from the noisy mission. He also liked the way the preacher explained the Bible.

When the choir stood to sing a special number, George Thompson pointed to a glowing young woman. "That's my sister, Helen, third seat, third row from the left." Billy saw the enthusiasm with which Helen sang, the dark brown eyes and black hair. He noticed she stood tall like a woman proud of her Lord. Even her face beamed with the earnestness of the words of the hymn she was singing. Billy decided he must see more of this young lady.

"I'd like to meet your sister sometime, George."

"Oh, her. Well, you could see her at prayer meeting. She is here every Wednesday night." George tossed the remark aside, but Billy stored it in his mind.

The next Wednesday night Billy finished practice early. He took a shower and put on his church clothes. Off he went to the Jefferson Park Presbyterian Church. He knew where there was a prayer meeting he wanted to attend.

After that he never missed a prayer meeting, Sunday morning, evening worship service, or

Sunday school hour unless he was speaking somewhere else.

Billy did meet Helen and soon was her escort in spite of a neighbor who thought Helen was his special friend. He didn't have to think of places to take her, because she wanted to be in church every time the door opened. Billy soon became interested in the church activities and joined the congregation.

Helen was elated. "Now Father will like you better." She said this hopefully, for her father did not like professional ball players.

Mr. Thompson soon found that Billy Sunday was no ordinary baseball player. Billy testified openly to being a Christian and maintained Christian standards. He talked to the others about drinking and coarse language. Most of all he yearned for others to love his Jesus.

Some reporters found out about his testimony and faithfully reported it in the newspapers. The baseball fans soon yelled encouraging words from the grandstands. Life was moving very fast for Billy.

Word of Billy Sunday's love for Christ and young people reached the sports administrator of Northwestern University in Chicago. He contacted Billy and asked him to coach the university baseball team in his spare time.

"I'll do it for you, if you will let me attend one of your classes," bargained Billy Sunday.

"What class is that?"

"Your class in elocution!" answered Billy. "I'm

always being asked to speak in public, and I really don't know how. I'd like to learn how to control my voice."

"We will see that you are enrolled at once, Mr. Sunday." He did see to it, and Billy attended classes for the school year of 1888 and 1889.

Along with playing ball for the White Stockings, courting Helen Thompson, and constantly attending church, Billy coached the Northwestern University team.

One of the first rules he made was: "No swearing on the baseball diamond, in the locker room, or in the dugout." This rule caused some members to be thrown off the team, some to choke back their words, and considerable relief for those who didn't want to take the name of the Lord in vain. Billy saw to it that every member learned to bat the ball. He couldn't help but wish he had had a coach who insisted he learn more than bunting.

On rare occasions when Billy was allowed to call on Helen Thompson in her parlor in Jefferson Park, George was gleeful. He loved to talk to Billy Sunday and rehash every play the team had made the week before. George and Billy talked while Helen sat sedately on the sofa and waited. Billy would look into Helen's deep brown eyes and forget what George was saying.

George finally realized that Billy's interest was in his sister. "How can I find out about the games if you are going to stare at Helen all the time?" complained George. "I need to be there. I mean, really there with the team. Could I, Billy? Could I come down to the dugout and get in on everything?"

This remark attracted Billy's attention. "Tell you what, George. I'll talk to the team about making you our mascot, if you will go for a walk or something."

"Oh, that would be great! It's a deal. The mascot of the Chicago White Stockings! Wow!"

After George was gone, Billy could say what was on his mind.

"Helen, will you marry me?"

Later Billy did talk to the team, and George Thompson was the mascot for several years. George also enjoyed taking credit for getting Billy and Helen together.

17

The Big Decision

In September 1888 Helen and Billy were married. Their honeymoon was a trip around the baseball circuit with the baseball team. Billy's teammates liked Helen at once. Her deep, soulful eyes and her Christian earnestness set her apart.

She loved seeing all the cities where the baseball games were played. She explored the historic spots, the shops, and even the churches of each city. This kept her busy during the long hours of baseball practice.

No matter where they were on Sunday, they attended church and spent the day away from the baseball world. They found a oneness of spirit and joy in belonging to each other that lasted all their lives.

More and more Billy Sunday was invited to tell his story. He stammered, he stumbled; he was undeniably a very poor speaker. The reason he was asked to speak was because he was a celebrated baseball player who loved Jesus. No matter how poorly he spoke, people listened. Each person felt as though he was speaking to him or to her alone. The audience sometimes helped him find a word when he stopped. They suffered when he couldn't think of any words to express what he was feeling. Each one knew, however, what his feelings were. They felt the wonder of God's love as he felt it—without any words. His honest blue eyes told what his lips could not say. He began to act out his meanings. When he did this he found everyone nodded and understood.

The Chicago Young Men's Christian Association found that they could get businessmen to come to fund-raising meetings by announcing that Billy Sunday would speak.

He would speak. Everyone would agree that it was the worst message they had ever heard. They stayed around for hours discussing what he had said, however, and the offerings were always good. After the message, Billy would talk individually with the men who came up to him. Many became Christians. No one could understand the remarkable results, least of all Billy Sunday.

Helen watched these results and began to pray. "Lord, lay Your hands on Billy. Bless him. Lord, have Your way with him." To Billy she quoted, "We do not know what the future holds, but we do know Who holds the future."

Billy signed big league baseball contracts with Pittsburgh and finally with Philadelphia. But that did not settle the unrest in Billy's soul.

The YMCA extended him an offer to work as a physical culture director, but Billy refused. "I may as well play baseball as teach baseball."

Later when the YMCA extended an offer to Billy Sunday to do Christian work, he considered it. Could he talk personally to men about Jesus? Could he secure speakers for noonday prayer meetings? Could he run the office? Raise money? Distribute literature? Could he visit the saloons and follow up on persons who had shown an interest? He thought about it. He prayed. He asked, "How can I know if God is calling me to His service?"

The team was ready to go on a baseball trip when Billy Sunday hurt his leg. To his surprise the doctor ordered him to stay off his leg and miss the trip and all the games. He was tempted to ignore the doctor. He was never one to show the white feather or shirk responsibility. Finally, however, he listened to Helen and the doctor and stayed home.

It was during this time that he read the Bible story about Gideon, who put out a fleece to help him make a decision. Billy decided to "put out a fleece" to see if he should go into Christian work or continue to play ball. Helen quoted, "God always gives the best to those who leave the choice to Him."

Billy sent a request to the Philadelphia ball club for a release from his contract. Rarely was anyone released before the season was over. In fact, not to finish a season was considered a disgrace. Billy knew he would never break his contract or his word. If he could get a release, however, that would be different. He set a date and prayed.

"Lord, if a release from my contract comes before March twenty-fifth, nineteen-oh-one, I'll quit baseball and go to work for You. If a release comes after the twenty-fifth I'll stick to baseball." Billy always talked to the Lord as though He were in the room. He always used plain English—even slang. Some people thought this was not respectful to the Lord, but Billy thought of God as some one you could talk to easily.

About that time there was an upset in the big leagues, and to everyone's surprise several teams disbanded. The Philadelphia team was one of them, and Billy's release came in the mail March 17.

Helen was thrilled. "You see, Billy, you put out the fleece and God answered. It wasn't just a coincidence this happened. God must want you to go into His service."

"That's the way it looks," answered Billy. "But look at this letter from the Cincinnati club. They heard about the upset and are offering me five hundred dollars a month to play ball for them."

"Five hundred a month!" Helen gasped. "And the YMCA is only offering eighty-three a month. Oh, Billy! What will you do?"

"Perhaps God is telling me to stay with baseball. You know we will soon have a baby to consider, and eighty-three dollars a month will hardly be enough to pay all our expenses."

They both prayed about it for days. Everyone they talked to advised Billy to play ball. Helen's father said, "You're crazy to hesitate! Sign the contract and play ball."

Finally the Cincinnati team set a date for a final answer.

The night before the date, Billy fell on his knees. He prayed and prayed. Helen tiptoed through the room. She told him dinner was ready. He didn't hear. Later, she tried again. "Billy, it is time to go to sleep." Still Billy didn't answer. He was lying prostrate on the rug still praying.

She left him on the floor and found him there the next morning. All around his body the rug was soaked in perspiration, but his prayer was complete. Helen saw a peace on Billy's face she had never seen there before.

"Billy, you've decided."

"Yes."

"Well, what are you going to do?"

"I'm going to follow Jesus, like I promised I would. It was really an easy decision when I finally trusted God to supply our needs."

"I'm glad." Helen smiled, and they put their arms around each other.

"I don't know why God wants me in His work. He knows I'm a good ball player and a poor preacher, but Grandfather always said, 'It's not the man of great natural talent who wins, but he

125

who pushes his talent, however small, to its utmost capacity!' I promised God last night I'll go where He wants me to go. I'll do what He wants me to do, and I'll be what He wants me to be! I mean it, Helen!"

18

First Experiences

It didn't take long for Billy Sunday to find out that his main job was managing the YMCA office. This kept him inside the building most of the day. He had to learn about the bookkeeping, how to keep track of the members and who had paid dues. Collecting dues from those who had not paid was very distasteful to him.

After years outside playing ball, the office routine was especially irksome. He prayed to God, questioning this confining work. Nevertheless, he struggled with it and learned the necessity of accounting for all money so that the workers could be paid. The salaries were small, but memberships were only five dollars a year, so there was never enough money. Sunday could see why the fund-raising luncheons for businessmen were necessary.

When Billy had been a speaker for those luncheons he felt his mission had been to reach the lost. Now, everything seemed different. The great need for money to pay salaries seemed to be the reason for fund-raising luncheons.

Billy solved the headache by asking one of the fine Christian women working in the bookkeeping department to be his assistant. He asked her to account for all the money and free him to do more important things. He appointed another Christian lady to do the scheduling of events at the YMCA. This freed him from another irksome task inside the office.

Little by little he began spending more time outside. Billy gave out literature on the street corners and talked to people as they passed. He invited to the "Y" anyone who showed an interest. There he explained the plan of salvation and led them to Jesus. He made a goal for himself to lead at least one person to Christ every day. Some of these people came to the "Y," but Billy found more of them on the streets, in saloons, cafés, or stores. Everywhere he went, he looked for unhappy faces and gave each person an invitation to be saved. Many accepted.

Each day became an adventure because he never knew what would happen from hour to hour. He spoke to the rich, the poor, the beggars, the working people. He listened to everyone. He heard the tale of woe of the brokenhearted. He looked into the eyes of the hard, mean, unfeeling individuals. He saw peace in the eyes of those who accepted Christ. He listened to their testimonies of joy and encouraged them to study the Bible.

One by one these individuals begged Billy to hold a Bible class to help them in the Christian life. He finally formed a class of converts and found that he, as the teacher, learned far more than any pupil. His teachers at the Jefferson Park Presbyterian Church were delighted to teach Bible lessons to Billy. He took the things he learned and taught them to his class of converts at the YMCA.

"I never saw anyone grow so steadily in every Christian way," Helen said. "He studies the Bible early and late. It seems he can't get enough of asking questions and learning about the Lord. I am so glad the Jefferson Park church elected him to be an elder."

As quickly as he learned a Bible doctrine he put it into practice himself and taught it to his class. People told him he would wear out if he kept up the pace he set. He laughed. "I'd rather wear out than rust out."

One person Billy could talk to about Bible questions was his new friend Peter Bilhorn. Other people tired of Billy's questions. Peter would listen carefully and explain. He showed him how the Bible fit together. "If you don't understand how differently God worked in different time periods, you will think the Bible contradicts itself."

Billy had a way of taking what he learned from the Bible and applying it to the average person. He said, "I want to give out the gospel so plainly that men can come from the factories and not have to bring along a dictionary." He did not comfort his converts. He aroused them to repent of sin, tell others of their salvation, and study the Bible. Mr. L. William Mener, head of the YMCA, was pleased.

After three years of experience doing personal work, managing the office at the YMCA, and arranging hundreds of meetings, Billy had exhausted all his savings. He found that his $83 salary was the last to be paid and often was months late in coming. He walked to work to save carfare, skipped lunch, wore his old clothes, and still was pinched to pay his rent and provide for his wife and two children.

At this time the Reverend J. Wilbur Chapman, well-known Presbyterian evangelist, invited Billy Sunday to become his "advance man." He was to go ahead of the evangelist to arrange meetings, to organize choirs, to advertise, and to erect the tent. During the meetings Billy was to sell song books and sermons, take up the offering, and substitute if Chapman was ill.

Billy prayed about this call to the service of the Lord. The evangelist promised Billy a share of the offering. "It certainly will be greater than eight-three dollars a month and expenses."

Helen was happy. She told their two children that God would use Daddy in a great way. Billy told them, "I want to be a giant for God. I believe in evangelism."

"Yes, we must have faith," responded Helen.

"Faith is the beginning of something of which you can't see the end, but in which you believe.

I don't see the end of this step, but I believe God wants me to take it."

Billy accepted the invitation and learned to be a "practical man." Every city they visited had problems. He alone was supposed to bring about unity among ministers of differing faiths. He alone was supposed to incite the populace to revival. He alone was supposed to organize prayer warriors. He soon found that he alone could do nothing. Only with God's help could he hope to accomplish anything. He learned to depend on the Lord and to give Him the credit. In the meantime he worked.

Sunday worked with the ministers of the cities in which the Chapman meetings were held. Often he found lip service and agreement among the pastors but very little real effort to promote the meetings. He wrote to Chapman, "Some preachers need the cushion of their chairs upholstered oftener than they need their shoes half-soled."

Sunday worked with the reporters. He publicly expressed appreciation for their cooperation. He provided free copies of Chapman's sermons and space for them to write their articles.

He worked with the tents and soon found problems. To discourage thieves, someone had to sleep in the tent at night. Billy hated the cold and the loneliness. Each night seemed like eternity. If a shower came in the middle of a Chapman meeting, folks would hurry away. Wind would sometimes blow the tent down, and Sunday was often seen pulling and tugging to get the canvas in place. Tents were heavy to move from city to city. Sunday struggled setting them up again in the next city. His ongoing war with tents left him disgusted. He wished never to see a tent again.

Mr. Chapman believed the converts at his meetings should be asked to join a local church and be instructed in Christian living. But when they came to the altar there was such a crowd that little could be done to help them.

Billy Sunday organized personal workers to meet with the converts in private tents behind the main tent. This often established a friendship that lasted for years.

J. Wilbur Chapman was very pleased with Billy Sunday's work. Mr. Chapman himself was always popular with the Presbyterians and recommended Billy for ordination into the ministry.

Billy Sunday had worked faithfully as an elder in the Jefferson Park Presbyterian Church for many years. He had been faithful to the teachings and doctrines of the church since he had joined in 1888. Because of this, the body of elders and the pastor agreed to an ordination service in 1903.

At the service the elders, pastor, and Mr. Chapman sat in a semi-circle, and Billy Sunday sat at the front of the assembly and answered questions fired at him by any member present.

Billy said, "I was on the hot seat, but God gave me the answers."

The group checked Billy's personal life to find any flaws that would make him an undesirable minister. They found none. They checked his knowledge of the Bible. Most of Billy's study had been private reading and memorization. They found that he could quote long passages of Scripture. He knew the answers to Bible questions and could explain doctrine. Everyone in the room agreed that he was sound in doctrine and learned in the Word of God.

When they asked him about his personal beliefs about evangelism and his commitment to God, they were more than pleased. Because they all felt he was a dedicated worker, they ordained him to the ministry of the Presbyterian church.

Helen was very pleased, and Billy was more determined than ever to do whatever God asked him to do. He still wondered what it would be.

19

God's Doors

New Year's day 1896 was a real holiday for Billy. He was enjoying his family, Helen and the two children. Little Helen, five years old, and George, two years old, were still talking about the Christmas holidays. Billy's mother had visited their home in Chicago. He enjoyed seeing his mother and children playing together and talking. He was thankful he had been able to help his mother as she grew older.

Billy laughed as he remembered little Helen's dismay when Grandma told on "Daddy." Billy had never told his wife about the time he had played out the story of George Washington in the family orchard. Grandma laughed. "You still can see the scars where Willie chopped at the apple tree. We never knew how the poor tree survived his attack. Willie was like George Washington. He came into the house and said he couldn't tell a lie, he chopped down the tree." Billy determined to go back home and see the scars one day.

Suddenly the door bell rang, and Billy found a young man who announced, "Telegram for Billy Sunday."

"I wonder what has gone wrong now!" he exclaimed. Ripping open the envelope he read: "Accepted call as pastor Bethany Church. All meetings cancelled. Rev. J. Wilbur Chapman."

Billy was stunned. He handed the telegram to Helen, who dropped into a chair exclaiming, "Oh, Billy! What will you do? If there are no meetings, you have no job. I don't understand how this could happen."

"Everywhere we hold meetings, we see groups of men from churches without pastors. Reverend Chapman has had calls before, but he always refused. I knew he was tired of traveling and missing his family, but I am surprised he stopped the meetings."

"Can you go back to the YMCA?"

"No, someone else is doing my job."

"Can you play baseball?"

"No, I promised God I would work for Him. I said I'd go where He wants me to go and do what He wants me to do."

"Billy, God never closes one door without opening another. He didn't bring you this far to desert you now. I know you are suffering, Billy, but out of suffering come the strongest souls. God's wounded make His best soldiers," quoted Helen.

They prayed. Again Billy prayed all night seeking God's will.

In the morning another telegram came. This time it was a request to conduct an evangelistic meeting in Garner, Iowa.

"But I don't know one person in Garner, Iowa!" marveled Billy. "How could they know about me?"

"Didn't you say people came from other towns to hear Chapman?"

"Yes, but Chapman is a well-known speaker. I'm not even a preacher."

"Oh, yes, you are!" contradicted his wife. "The Presbytery has ordained you, you know."

"But I don't have any sermons. You can't preach without sermons."

"What did you do when Reverend Chapman was ill and you took his place?"

"Well, I just said what he said. I'd heard it a hundred times."

"Couldn't you do that in Iowa?"

"Not without asking him, I wouldn't."

Mr. Chapman gave Billy permission to use any of his messages. Since he always had printed copies for sale, Billy had no trouble finding many sermons.

He selected eight sermons and set out for Garner, Iowa. He went with fear and trembling, telling himself, *God never says, "Forward," without leading the way.*

The people in Garner, Iowa, were very pleased with the meetings. The results shocked the town. People attended Billy's campaign who never went to church. Drunkards were saved and quit drinking. Erring husbands were saved and returned home. Robbers were saved and returned their stolen goods. The city was turned upside down for Jesus. Billy wrote to his wife, "This is the Lord's doing; it is marvelous in our eyes."

Only Billy Sunday was dissatisfied. He tried to preach exactly like J. Wilbur Chapman because that seemed right. But he found it very difficult to say another's words and to assume another's manner. When he would forget about the sermon and see the hunger in the eyes of the people, he could be himself. He felt the people respond even more when he acted out a scene. Mr. Chapman had never done that, but then Mr. Chapman had never been at a complete loss for words.

Before the meetings in Garner were over, Billy Sunday received two more invitations for meetings. From that time he always had more invitations than he could possibly accept. Billy counted each invitation as a signal from God to continue in evangelism. At last he knew what God wanted him to do. Years later he said, "I have tried to be true to the Lord and to do just what He wants me to do." He always said it was no power of his that achieved great results. He repeated over and over again, "This is the Lord's doing."

God showed Billy that he didn't have to be a J. Wilbur Chapman to succeed with the common people. He gave him confidence to preach in his own way. His way was with slang, snappy sayings, and downright scolding for sin. The people loved it. No one moved, talked, or looked around when Billy was acting and speaking. Even the children were spellbound.

The day came when J. Wilbur Chapman came to hear Billy Sunday preach one of "his" sermons. He said, "I didn't recognize the sermon at all, so changed was the wording and manner of delivery. No one can ever accuse Billy of preaching like anyone else. He is God's man, preaching God's way as no one else ever did."

Billy Sunday gathered a team of helpers about him. He had an advance man to go ahead and make preparations. He found excellent song leaders such as Homer A. Rodeheaver. He insisted on building "tabernacles" instead of struggling with tents. Some of the tabernacles covered a city block and seated more than two million persons. He insisted that all the ministers in a city invite him before he accepted a call to come and preach. He organized personal workers. He cooperated with the newspapers, and many a reporter came as a scoffer and went home as a Christian.

Billy's meetings were held in the Midwest during his early years. People said, "Billy Sunday may do for the Middle West, but the East will not stand him."

To everyone's great surprise Sunday's greatest meetings were held in Pittsburgh, Scranton, Philadelphia, Baltimore, Boston, and New York.

Many meetings lasted two to six months with full attendance. His converts numbered about four hundred thousand.

Helen Sunday became "Ma Sunday" to millions of people. She traveled with Billy to the meetings and attended to his clothes and meals with care. She was also the business manager of the team. She saw that offerings were spent wisely and judiciously. It was Ma Sunday who paid bills and put aside savings for leaner days. She said, "Money is a good servant but a poor master."

Without Helen, Billy would have been burdened with details that would have detracted from his work for the Lord. He never answered when people criticized him. He remembered Mrs. Scott's words, "Just don't open your mouth."

When Billy Sunday went to a city he didn't preach only in the tabernacles. He went to manufacturing shops and spoke to workers as they ate lunch. He gathered business people for luncheon meetings. He held services in schools, in jails, in hospitals. He even gathered social leaders for afternoon parlor meetings. Everywhere he preached against sin and invited the people to believe in Christ. Billy Sunday spared no effort in reaching everybody in the city for Jesus.

The president of the United States greeted him when he went to Washington, D.C. *American Magazine* held a voting contest throughout the United States. The question was: "Who's the greatest man in America?" To Billy Sunday's astonishment he was voted the eighth greatest man along with Andrew Carnegie and Judge Lindsey. In June 1912 Dr. Robert McWatty, president of Westminister College at New Wilmington, Pennsylvania, conferred an honorary degree of Doctor of Divinity on Billy Sunday. Billy was not present because he was holding a campaign in Beaver Falls. Somehow Billy never felt like writing D.D. after his name, although to have that degree was a great honor.

Billy Sunday never considered himself great. He always felt he was a poor preacher and said, "Don't get chesty over success." He never had his own plan for his life. He admitted, "I have just gone along, entering doors that the Lord has opened one after another."

But Billy Sunday always pushed. He followed Squire Corley's advice, "It is not the man of great natural talent who wins, but he who pushes his talent, however small, to its utmost capacity."

Glossary

In order of appearance in the story:

twenty-three skiddoo	*leave in a hurry, disappear*
faster than greased lightning	*extremely swift*
in the buff	*naked*
get off your high horse	*don't be so proud or self-important*
to have frolic on the brain	*to be thinking of play, not work*
to paddle one's own canoe	*do your own thing*
doesn't know beans	*ignorant*
the die is cast	*things cannot be changed now*
beats the Dutch	*unbelievable, amazing*
to walk the chalk	*behave, toe the line*
gone to Jericho	*"spaced out," crazy*
swallowed hook, line, and sinker	*he fell for it*
takes the cake	*the best*
thinks he's the goods	*hot shot, proud of himself*
to "connect," in baseball	*hit the ball hard*
show the white feather	*chicken out*
put out a fleece	*a way of finding God's will (see Judges 6-7 in the Bible)*